The New Grammar in Action 3

Barbara H. Foley

and Elizabeth R. Neblett

with Deborah Singer Pires

Union County College
Cranford, New Jersey

Heinle & Heinle Publishers
I(T)P An International Thomson Publishing Company
Boston, Massachusetts 02116 U.S.A.

ACKNOWLEDGMENTS We wish to thank the faculty and students at the Institute for Intensive English, Union County College, New Jersey, for their support and encouragement during this project. Many faculty members previewed the units in their classrooms, offering suggestions for changes and additions. Students shared stories and compositions, and smiled and posed for numerous photographs. Paulette Koubek Yao and her students at Hong Kong University, and Luca Girardini provided information about university education in Hong Kong and Italy, respectively. Robin Cannata contributed the photograph and story of his grandmother's life. Thanks, also, to the staff at Heinle & Heinle, who remained encouraging and calm throughout the development and production of this revision.

The publication of *The New Grammar in Action 3* was directed by the members of the Heinle & Heinle Secondary and Adult ESL Publishing Team:

Managing Developmental Editor:	Amy Lawler
Production Services Coordinator:	Maryellen E. Killeen
Market Development Directors:	Jonathan Boggs and Thomas Dare

Also participating in the publication of the program were:

Vice President and Publisher, ESL:	Stanley Galek
Associate Developmental Editor:	Joyce La Tulippe
Director of Global ELT Training:	Evelyn Nelson
Manufacturing Coordinator:	Mary Beth Hennebury
Project Manager:	Hockett Editorial Service
Photo/Video Specialist:	Jonathan Stark
Interior Designer/Compositor:	Greta D. Sibley & Associates
Cover Designer:	Gina Petti/Rotunda Design House
Illustrator:	James Edwards

Manufactured in the United States of America.

ISBN: 08384-67288   **10 9 8 7 6 5**

Heinle & Heinle is a division of International Thomson Publishing, Inc.

Library of Congress Cataloging-in-Publication Data
Foley, Barbara H.
    The new grammar in action : an illustrated workbook / Barbara H.
Foley with Elizabeth R. Neblett.
        p.   cm.
    ISBN 0-8384-6728-8
    1. English language--Textbooks for foreign speakers.   2. English
language--Grammar--Problems, exercises, etc.   I. Neblett, Elizabeth
R.
PE1128.F568   1998
428.2'4--dc21   98-19886
                                              CIP

Photo Credits Photos by Elizabeth R. Neblett on pages 2, 19, 32, 58, 83, 106. Other photos by Jonathan Stark, Bettman Archive, Stock Boston, Sygma, and The Stock Market.

■ Contents

To the Teacher

The New Grammar in Action, a three-level grammar series for secondary and adult ESL/EFL students, offers a dynamic, communicative approach to language learning. The third book of the series is aimed at the intermediate student. The series presents English language structure and practice through inviting contexts such as education, job performance, business and industry, and country music. Bold, lively illustrations, authentic student photographs, and information-rich charts and graphs illustrate each context for practice and use of the structural focus. The series offers a variety of exercises for students and teachers to engage in both whole class and small-group activities. Listening components to each unit guide students to identify structures in context and in use, progressing from controlled presentation to more open-ended, interactive language use. Throughout the text, students are encouraged to share their ideas and experiences, to think more critically about subject matter, comparing and contrasting ideas as they gain greater control and confidence in the target language.

GRAMMAR IN ACTION

Grammar in Action sections open each unit, setting the context and grammar focus. Listening or reading activities, accompanied by illustrations, introduce a new topic and related vocabulary. Before listening to the tape, students may be asked to make predictions about what they are about to hear. Students may ask to hear the listening as many times as they wish. Listening sections are structured to allow students the opportunity to follow pictures in sequence, identify words and phrases, fill in information, and comprehend natural language forms in use.

Activities in the **Grammar in Action** section are varied for whole class and pair oriented work, appealing to diverse learning styles. The activities direct students to answer questions, complete sentences, provide information about themselves, form sentences from cues, give directions and describe illustrations. In this way, **Grammar in Action** units set the tone for high student interest and interaction during classroom time.

WORKING TOGETHER

Working Together sections give students the opportunity to work with a partner or a small group on more open-ended, communicative exercises presented within the context of the unit. Grammar is put into immediate use in the form of interviews, surveys, and role plays as well as problem-solving activities. Students are encouraged towards fluency with the exchange of ideas.

Information gap exercises, identified as **Student to Student** sections, are included throughout many of the **Working Together** units. These sections allow for both controlled and open-ended practice between students. Students work in pairs, each looking at a different page. Students share and exchange ideas through challenging exercises that ask them to find information, match questions and answers, and think about a topic in new ways.

PRACTICING ON YOUR OWN

Practicing on Your Own sections allow students the time to internalize the structures presented within each unit through written practice and expression. This section is useful for individual homework and review. Students gain more confidence writing and thinking in the target language as they complete a variety of exercises. In addition, there is ample tense contrast and question formation practice.

SHARING OUR STORIES

Many units include **Sharing Our Stories** sections with authentic essays and narratives by and about ESL students and their experiences. These personal narratives are points of departure to stimulate student story-telling and writing. After reading these stories, students are encouraged to write about their own lives and experiences. Additionally, there are other opportunities presented throughout the text, marked by a writing icon, for students to expand on a topic or idea through their own personal written expression.

HAVING FUN WITH THE LANGUAGE

The **Having Fun with the Language** section outlines expansion activities for both in and outside of class time. Suggestions for surveys, games, interviews, and research and library work give students the chance to use the language in new contexts. Students and teachers alike can select activities of high interest and appeal.

GRAMMAR SUMMARY

These sections offer additional structural focus throughout each unit by providing an overview of the grammar for the lesson. Explanations are brief and clear, appropriate for intermediate students. Appendices at the back of the book offer additional support and reference material.

Teachers will view *The New Grammar in Action* as both a solid basis for classroom instruction and a text which allows for creative expansion of grammar structures in form and use. Over time, teachers will personalize their use of the series, expanding the units with current magazine articles, charts from newspapers, workshop ideas, and more.

CORRELATIONS

The New Grammar in Action is correlated to the following Heinle & Heinle products: *Making Connections, Levels 1–3; Crossroads Café Books A & B; Voices in Literature: Bronze, Silver, and Gold Levels;* and *Grammar 3D* grammar software.

The New Grammar in Action 3

 **Education**

Present Continuous Tense; Simple Present Tense

Grammar in Action

Present Continuous

■ **A. SCHOOL DAYS** *Look at the pictures below. Use the present continuous tense to describe what is happening in each of the pictures.*

> **EXAMPLE**
>
> A student **is talking** on the telephone.
> The students **are taking** a test.

Present Continuous Tense		
I	am	
	am not	
He	is	
She	isn't	studying.
They	are	
You	aren't	

■ B. PRESENT CONTINUOUS *Read the following sentences about the pictures on page 2. Fill in the blanks with a verb in the present continuous tense.*

1. Some students _are sitting_____ at a table in the cafeteria.

2. They _____ a short break.

3. A few students _____ coffee.

4. They _____ about their class.

5. One student _____ a telephone call.

6. She _____ to her boyfriend.

7. She _____ in the hall.

8. The students in another class _____ a test.

9. One student _____ about the answer.

10. Other students _____ their answers on the test.

■ C. MY CLASSROOM *Look around your classroom and answer the following questions. Write the name of the person in the blank. (The answer can be this: **No one is.**)*

1. Who is sitting next to the door?   _____

2. Who is sharpening a pencil?   _____

3. Who is talking to the teacher?   _____

4. Who is reading?   _____

5. Who is sitting in the front of the room?   _____

6. Who is wearing a suit?   _____

7. Who is sitting next to you?   _____

8. Who is drinking a beverage?   _____

9. Who is wearing glasses?   _____

10. Who is writing something?   _____

A. LISTEN: THE UNIVERSITY OF TEXAS AT SAN ANTONIO

Listen to the description of this university. As you listen, circle or fill in the correct information.

Location: urban   suburban   rural

Degrees: two-year   four-year

Type of university: public   private

Number of students:

_____ full time

_____ part time

_____ graduate

Number of faculty: more than _____

Application fee: $_____

Recommendations for high school applicants:

_____ years of English

_____ years of a foreign language

_____ years of math

_____ years of social science

_____ years of lab science

_____ years of fine arts

Three majors: _____ _____ _____

Services:

_____ counseling and _____ service

_____ at the Learning Center

Freshman _____

A.A.   B.A.   M.A.   A.S.   B.S.   Ph.D.
Which degrees are two-year degrees?
Which degrees are four-year degrees?
Which degrees are graduate degrees?

■ B. TRUE OR FALSE *Read each statement and circle **T** for true, or **F** for false.*

T   F   1. The University of Texas at San Antonio is a four-year university.

T   F   2. U.T.S.A. is a private university.

T   F   3. The university is in downtown San Antonio.

T   F   4. U.T.S.A. has a graduate school.

T   F   5. U.T.S.A. employs more than eight hundred faculty.

T   F   6. Students pay $15 for the application fee.

T   F   7. The university recommends two years of a foreign language.

T   F   8. The university recommends one year of fine arts.

T   F   9. Undergraduates choose from many different majors.

Present Tense		
I		
You		
We	study	
They		biology.
He		
She	studies	

Present Tense: *have*		
I		
You		
We	have	
They		a computer.
He		
She	has	
It		

■ C. UNIVERSITY LIFE *Fill in the correct present tense of the verb in parentheses.*

1. The University of Texas at San Antonio _____ (have) many campuses.

2. 9,400 students _____ (study) at U.T.S.A.

3. High school students _____ (pay) an application fee.

4. U.T.S.A. _____ (offer) science and humanities courses.

5. Students _____ (complete) three years of high school math and two years of social science before they go to U.T.S.A.

6. U.T.S.A. _____ (have) a learning center with tutors and counselors for the students.

7. The university _____ (give) the students free career counseling.

8. Students _____ (go) to the employment service when they _____ (need) to find jobs.

9. Students with disabilities _____ (receive) special services from the university.

10. The university _____ (hold) an orientation for new students.

5

■ D. NEGATIVES: THE ROOMMATES *Sophie and Lizzy are college roommates, but they have very different schedules, habits, and interests. Read each sentence about Sophie; then tell how Lizzy is different.*

Present Tense: Negatives		
I		
You	don't study	
They		biology.
He	doesn't study	
She		

EXAMPLE

Sophie belongs to the science club. (Lizzy—photography club)

Lizzy doesn't belong to the science club. She belongs to the photography club.

Sophie	Lizzy
1. Sophie has all her courses in the morning.	(in the afternoon)
2. Sophie takes science courses.	(humanities courses)
3. Sophie studies in the library.	(in her room)
4. Sophie works in the biology lab.	(in the dining hall)
5. Sophie likes to work on the computer.	(write by hand)
6. Sophie hands in her work on time.	(late)
7. Sophie gets up early in the morning.	(sleep late)
8. Sophie eats a lot of health food.	(fast food)
9. Sophie keeps her part of the room neat.	(messy)

Do you have a roommate?
How are you the same?
How are you different?

■ E. DO/DOES QUESTIONS *Complete these questions with **Do** or **Does**; then write the short answer.*

Do / Does Questions
Do you work?
 Yes, I **do**.   No, I **don't**.
Does she work?
 Yes, she **does**.   No, she **doesn't**.

1. __Does__ Sophie take all of her courses in the morning?   _Yes, she does._

2. _____ you take all of your courses in the morning?   _____

3. _____ Lizzie study in the library?   _____

4. _____ you study in the library?   _____

5. _____ Sophie like to work on the computer?   _____

6. _____ you like to work on the computer?   _____

7. _____ Sophie get up early?   _____

8. _____ you get up early?   _____

9. _____ Sophie hand in her work on time?   _____

10. _____ you hand in your work on time?   _____

F. QUESTIONS: THE SCHEDULE
Chen is a pre-med student. Form questions about his schedule with the cues below.

	M	T	W	Th	F
7:00		Works in the dining hall		Works in the dining hall	
8:00					
9:00	English Comp	Chemistry Lecture	English Comp	Chemistry Lecture	English Comp
10:00	Biology Lecture		Biology Lecture		Biology Lecture
11:00					
12:00					
1:00	Psychology		Psychology	Chemistry Lab	Psychology
2:00	Biology Lab				Writing Lab
3:00					
4:00			Band Practice		
5:00					

EXAMPLE

Chen / work in the library?

Does Chen work in the library?

No, he doesn't.

When / he / have band practice?

When does he have band practice?

He has band practice on Wednesdays from 4:00 to 6:00.

1. Chen / work in the dining hall?
2. you / work / on campus?
3. he / have English on Wednesday?
4. you / have English on Wednesday?
5. he / take classes on Friday afternoon?
6. he / take two science courses?
7. What time / he / take / psychology?
8. What / he / do on Wednesday afternoons?
9. What day / he / have free time in the afternoon?
10. What time / his classes / begin on Monday, Wednesday, and Friday?
11. When / his classes / end on Friday?
12. What time / your classes / end?

Present Tense: Questions			
When	do	I you they	study?
What	does	he she	

■ G. *WHO* QUESTIONS *Answer these* **who** *questions about students in your class.*

1. Who always arrives on time?
2. Who wears a baseball cap to class?
3. Who often arrives late?
4. Who never has a pencil?
5. Who goes to work after class?
6. Who plays on a team?
7. Who talks the most?
8. Who asks the most questions?

Who Questions	
Who	works at school?
	has a computer?
	studies biology?

Write two more *who* questions about your classmates.

■ H. ADVERBS OF FREQUENCY: MY TEACHER *Talk about your teacher, using the adverbs of frequency.*

Place adverbs of frequency **before the verb.**
  He *always* **comes** to school late.
  She *seldom* **walks** to school.
Place adverbs of frequency **after be.**
  He **is** *never* late.
  She **is** *often* tired.

EXAMPLE

speak loudly

My teacher **almost always** speaks loudly.

1. speak softly
2. (be) on time
3. give quizzes
4. use red ink to correct our papers
5. write on the blackboard
6. give us homework on the weekends
7. (be) quiet
8. use a tape recorder
9. show videos
10. (be) strict

Adverbs of Frequency

100%	always
	frequently
	often
	sometimes
	seldom
	rarely
	hardly ever
0%	never

I. NON-ACTION VERBS *Study this list of non-action verbs.*

Non-Action Verbs

The following verbs usually take the simple present.

appear	have	like	own	sound
believe	hear	look	prefer	taste
feel	hope	love	see	understand
hate	know	need	smell	want

Make sentences about the students in the picture, using the following cues. Be careful—many of the verbs are non-action verbs.

1. Students / like / to meet / student center
2. They / need to relax / between classes
3. Two students / play / video games
4. Some students / study / together
5. They / prefer to study / student center
6. They / hope to pass / test today
7. They / (not) hear / the noise
8. Lana and her boyfriend / watch / TV
9. Bill, her boyfriend, / look / bored
10. He / (not) like / soap operas
11. Two students / buy / pizza
12. The pizza / smell / good

J. THE CHESS PLAYERS
Read this story about the two chess players in the picture. Fill in the correct form of the verbs in parentheses: present or present continuous.

Lee and Jamal are juniors in the computer science department. They <u>always study</u> (study / always) hard, but every day they _____ (take) a break to play their favorite game—chess. Lee and Jamal _____ (prefer) chess to any other game.

Lee and Jamal _____ (play) chess almost every afternoon at 3:00. It's 4:30 now, and, as usual, they _____ (play) a game. Right now, Lee _____ (think) about his next move, and Jamal _____ (smile). He _____ (know) that he is about to win. Even though the student center is noisy, and all around them the students _____ (talk) and _____ (laugh), Lee _____ (negative—hear) anything. He _____ (concentrate) on the chess game. He _____ (want) to win.

Write a paragraph about another student or students in the picture. Use the present tense and the present continuous tense.

Working Together

A. UNIVERSITIES *Complete these sentences about universities in your country.*

1. It **is**   **isn't**   easy to get into a university in _____ .
   (name of country)
2. Tuition   **costs**   **doesn't cost**   a lot of money.
3. A typical university student   **goes**   **doesn't go**   to classes every day.
4. A typical student takes _____ courses a semester.
5. A typical student   **lives**   **doesn't live**   in a dormitory.
6. Students   **call**   **don't call**   professors by their first names.
7. Universities   **have**   **don't have**   good computer facilities.
8. During their college years, most students   **participate**   **don't participate**   in clubs or on athletic teams.
9. University professors   **give**   **don't give**   written exams.
10. Most students   **graduate**   **don't graduate**   after four or five years of study.

Read your sentences to a group of three or four students. Compare colleges in your countries. Then ask one another the questions on the next page.

1. When does the school year begin?
2. Do students take tests to enter a university?
3. What kind of tests do they take to enter a university?
4. Which university do most people consider the best? Why do they think so?
5. Who helps students select universities?
6. Do universities offer evening classes?
7. Do some students attend part time?
8. How often does a typical class meet?
9. Where do most students study?
10. Do university graduates find jobs easily after graduation?

■ B. STUDY HABITS

*How do you study? Read each statement and check **always**, **sometimes**, or **never** about your own study habits. Then listen and check the appropriate column as your partner describes his or her study habits.*

	Me			My Partner		
	ALWAYS	SOMETIMES	NEVER	ALWAYS	SOMETIMES	NEVER
1. I do my homework.	❑	❑	❑	❑	❑	❑
2. My homework is neat.	❑	❑	❑	❑	❑	❑
3. I ask questions in class.	❑	❑	❑	❑	❑	❑
4. I read a newspaper in English.	❑	❑	❑	❑	❑	❑
5. I try to speak English outside of class.	❑	❑	❑	❑	❑	❑
6. I keep my class work and papers organized.	❑	❑	❑	❑	❑	❑
7. I get to class on time.	❑	❑	❑	❑	❑	❑
8. I ask for extra help when I need it.	❑	❑	❑	❑	❑	❑
9. I speak English in class.	❑	❑	❑	❑	❑	❑
10. I study in a quiet place.	❑	❑	❑	❑	❑	❑
11. I use the library.	❑	❑	❑	❑	❑	❑
12. I use a dictionary when I study.	❑	❑	❑	❑	❑	❑
13. I study an hour a day or more.	❑	❑	❑	❑	❑	❑

Complete the following sentences about you and your partner.

1. My partner always _____ .

2. I never _____ .

3. Sometimes my partner and I _____ .

4. We never / always _____ .

> After reviewing the list, how could
> you improve your study time? Do you
> have any suggestions for your partner?

■ C. TWO STUDENTS *Steve is an excellent student and has a B average in college. Jake is a lazy student and is on probation. Make a list of the reasons why everyone says that Steve is hardworking. Then make a list of the reasons why everyone says that Jake is lazy.*

Steve

1. Steve reviews his notes after every class. _____

2. _____

3. _____

4. _____

5. _____

Jake

1. Jake never studies until the day before a test. _____

2. _____

3. _____

4. _____

5. _____

D. STUDENT TO STUDENT
Marisa takes the seven classes listed in the box below. **Student A** *and* **Student B** *both have information about Marisa's schedule. Read your statements to each other, but do not look at each other's books. Figure out Marisa's schedule and write each class next to the correct time.*

Student A: Turn to page 189.
Student B: Turn to page 190.

SCHEDULE

7:45   Homeroom _____

8:00   _____

9:00   _____

10:00   _____

11:00   _____

12:00   _____

1:00   _____

2:00   _____

Classes
Biology
French
American history
Gym
Calculus
English
Lunch

Practicing on Your Own

A. PRESENT TENSE: STUDENTS AROUND THE WORLD
Fill in the correct form of the verb in parentheses.

Korea

1. The Korean Ministry of Education ___always prepares___ (prepare / always) the entrance exams.

2. The universities _____ (evaluate) the students according to their entrance exams, test scores, high school grades, and overall scholastic ability. They _____ (negative—pay) as much attention to extracurricular activities and teacher recommendations as U.S. universities do.

3. Korean students _____ (live / sometimes) in apartments near the university campus, but others _____ (live) at home with their families.

Hong Kong

1. A student in Hong Kong usually _____ (select) a major before she _____ (apply) to college. Then the student _____ (take) an "A-level" exam. The results _____ (go) to the universities that the student has selected. If the student's score _____ (be—negative) good enough, the student may have to change majors in order to study at that school.

2. University students in Hong Kong _____ (have) the same six to eight classes the entire school year. They _____ (negative—change) at the end of semesters as in the United States.

3. University students in Hong Kong _____ (have) to take many required courses.

4. It _____ (be) very difficult to change majors. Most students _____ (focus) on their future careers when they _____ (select) a major.

Italy

1. Italian students _____ (take) entrance exams to enter a specific department because many departments have too many students and cannot accept all the students who apply.

2. A typical Italian student _____ (live) in an apartment or at home.

3. Italian students often _____ (study) independently because the lectures _____ (be) very full. They _____ (negative—attend) lectures every day. Instead, they _____ (study) from the textbooks because most exams _____ (test) only the information in the books.

4. Required attendance _____ (depend) on department. For example, engineering students _____ (go / usually) to class every day. Literature students _____ (negative—attend) all the lectures; they can study at home.

5. A typical Italian student who _____ (be) a humanities major _____ (take / usually) oral exams. In other subjects, professors _____ (give / often) written exams.

■ B. QUESTIONS: AMERICAN UNIVERSITIES *Use the present tense and complete these questions and answers about American universities.*

1. __Do_____ all American professors __give_____ (give) lectures?

   No, they __don't_____ . Some professors __lead_____ (lead) small-group discussions.

2. _____ American students _____ (have) to buy textbooks?

   Yes, they _____ , and books _____ (cost / often) a lot of money.

3. _____ American courses _____ (have) a lot of students?

   Yes, they _____ . Popular courses, such as biology and history,

   _____ (have / often) more than 300 students in large lecture halls.

4. _____ students _____ (ask) professors questions during the lecture?

   Sometimes they _____ , and sometimes they _____ . It _____
   (depend) on the student and the professor.

5. What kind of exams _____ students _____ (take / usually)?

   Students _____ (have) to take written exams, and they _____
   (take / almost always) a mid-semester and a final exam. A typical humanities professor

   _____ (require / often) one or more typed papers during the semester.

6. Who _____ (help) students who are having trouble with the course?

   Tutors, teaching assistants, and the professors _____ (help) students in the learning

   centers or in their offices.

7. Who _____ (advise) students on career opportunities?

   The counselors _____ . Also, companies _____ (visit / often)

   college campuses to recruit students.

■ C. QUESTIONS *Read the information and complete the questions.*

New Jersey Institute of Technology

New Jersey Institute of Technology, or N.J.I.T., is located in Newark, New Jersey, ten miles from New York City. It is a four-year public university and technical college. The college offers bachelor's degrees in science, business, and technology. N.J.I.T. also has graduate programs. The college requires interested students to have four years of high school

English and two years of science, including one of a laboratory science. Different majors, such as management, require three years of high school mathematics. Students also take the SAT I (Scholastic Aptitude Test). Ninety percent of the students come from New Jersey and 70% commute between home and school. The average age of entering students is eighteen.

In addition to day classes, N.J.I.T. offers many evening and early morning classes, and it also has a summer session. Students who need extra preparation get special instruction, English as a second language classes, or tutoring. Like many other colleges today, N.J.I.T. has telecourses and on-line courses for students who want to study from home. N.J.I.T. gives each student a personal computer for use until graduation. The students can purchase the computers at graduation.

On campus, students live in dormitories. There is also fraternity housing for students who are members of various fraternities. For fun, students write for the student newspaper, join the musical theater group, or join another of the cultural, social, athletic, or service organizations.

Raji is in his second year at N.J.I.T. He has a full schedule and he works in the computer center three times a week. Right now, he's in the student center, studying for a math test. He and his friends are reviewing together. They're solving problems and discussing the solutions. They all want to get high scores on the test.

1. Where _is NJIT?_____ In Newark, New Jersey.

2. What degrees _____? Bachelor's and graduate degrees.

3. Does _____? Yes, it does.

4. What test _____? The SAT I.

5. What percent of the students _____? 90%.

6. Who _____? N.J.I.T. does.

7. What special courses _____? Tele-courses and on-line courses.

8. What _____? A personal computer.

9. Where _____? In the dormitories.

10. Do _____? Yes, they do.

11. Where _____? In the student center.

12. Who _____? With his friends.

13. Why _____? They want to get high scores.

▪ D. ACTION AND NON-ACTION VERBS *Complete this story with the verb in the present tense or present continuous tense.*

Joe is the manager of the student center, and this is his twentieth year working there.

Joe _____ (know) the names of almost all of the students who _____ (visit)

the center every day. He _____ (like) to talk to the students, and he _____

(miss) them during vacations.

Today is the beginning of final exams, so the student center _____ (negative—be)

as busy as usual. A few students _____ (talk) in a corner, soft music _____

(play), and a group of students _____ (discuss) a final project. A lot of the stu-

dents _____ (study) in the library this week and _____ (type) their papers in

the computer centers. Today, Joe _____ (prepare) some special events for the stu-

dents because he _____ (understand) that exam time is very stressful. The stu-

dents _____ (negative—have) a lot of free time during exam weeks, and they

_____ (miss / often) their meals at the dining hall. Joe _____ (keep) the cen-

ter open until 3:00 a.m. because he _____ (realize) that many students study all

night.

It's 11:30 p.m., and Joe _____ (make) the students' favorite cookies, and pizzas

_____ (bake) in the ovens. The center _____ (smell) wonderful. Students

_____ (begin) to look up from their books and _____ (get) ready to take a

study break.

Read Daniel's description of two college programs.

My brother Javier and I are studying for careers in the health field. My brother attends a four-year public college. He's a third year student, majoring in medical technology. He's doing his clinicals this year. He works eight hours a day, five days a week, in the medical technology department of a major hospital. He gets up at 4:00 in the morning because he has to be at the hospital by 5:00. He goes around to the different floors and takes blood from patients. Then he tests it in the laboratory. In the late afternoon and evening, he takes courses in advanced chemistry and microbiology.

I attend a community college and am more than halfway toward my nursing degree. I don't have any free time from early morning to 11:00 every night. I'm a part-time student because I have to work to have money for tuition. I have my clinicals in a hospital three mornings a week. I take three courses: microbiology, sociology, and anatomy and physiology. I also work forty hours a week at a restaurant. I'm so busy that I don't even have time to have a girlfriend! I hope to have both my registered nurse degree and my A.S. degree in two more years.

Daniel Urquia, Honduras

 Write about your educational plans. Are you in high school? Are you in college? What is your major? Describe your schedule. What are your plans for the future?

Having Fun with the Language

A. WHAT'S HAPPENING *With a group of four or five classmates, go to a place in your school where students meet. For example, visit the cafeteria, the computer lab, learning or tutoring center, or the gymnasium. Spend about fifteen minutes there, and quietly take notes. With your group, write a paragraph about what's happening. What are the people doing? Then go back to your class and read your report to your classmates.*

B. COLLEGE GUIDES *Visit your school library and find a popular college guide, such as Lovejoy's, Peterson's, or Barron's. Find information about a college you are interested in. Report your information to a group of classmates. Include the following information:*

Location	Three majors or departments
Number of students	Services
Admission requirements	Housing arrangements
Tuition and fees	Reasons that you like the college

Grammar Summary

I. Present continuous tense

We use the present continuous tense to talk about an action that is happening now.

Time expressions: **now**   **right now**   **at this moment**   **at the present time**

She **is studying** business.

Is she **studying** business?

Yes, she **is**.

Where **is** she **studying**?

She **is studying** at the University of Texas.

Who **is studying** biology?

Yolanda **is**.

■ 2. Present tense

We use the present tense to describe a routine or habitual action.

Time expressions:
    every day   **on the weekends**
    every week   **on Mondays**
    every year

Present tense	Present tense, third person singular
I **take** art.	He **takes** art.
Do you **take** art? Yes, I **do**.	**Does** he **take** art? Yes, he **does**.
When **do** you **take** art?	When d**oes** he **take** art?
Who **takes** art? I **do**.	Who **takes** art? He **does**.
They **take** art.	
Do they **take** art? Yes, they **do**.	
When **do** they **take** art?	
Who **takes** art? They **do**.	

■ 3. Adverbs of frequency

Place adverbs of frequency before the verb.

He *always* **comes** late.

Place adverbs of frequency after the verb *be*.

He *is* **always** late.

■ 4. Non-action verbs

Non-action verbs usually take the present tense form.

This exercise is easy. I **know** all the answers.

She's studying hard. She **wants** to do well on the test.

Colonial Times (1607–1776)

Past Tense; *Used to*

Look at the map of the United States. Where were the first colonies?

A. LISTEN *Look at the pairs of pictures and listen to the comparison between life in colonial times and life today. Then read each statement about colonial times. Circle **T** for true or **F** for false.*

T	F	1.	People went to the supermarket.
T	F	2.	People cooked on stoves.
T	F	3.	People milked their own cows.
T	F	4.	People used candles.
T	F	5.	People slept on mattresses and box springs.
T	F	6.	People talked to friends on telephones.
T	F	7.	Families watched television together.
T	F	8.	People drove cars from place to place.

Past Tense

I You We	watched didn't watch	TV.
He She They	drove didn't drive	a car.

B. NEGATIVES *Circle the correct verb.*

1. Colonial people   **watched   didn't watch**   television.

2. Colonial people   **grew   didn't grow**   their own food.

3. Colonial people   **milked   didn't milk**   cows.

4. Colonial people   **drove   didn't drive**   cars.

5. Colonial people   **wrote   didn't write**   letters.

6. Colonial people   **made   didn't make**   their own clothes.

7. Colonial women   **cooked   didn't cook**   over open fires.

8. Colonial children   **studied   didn't study**   in one-room schoolhouses.

9. Colonial people   **used   didn't use**   candles for light.

10. Colonial people   **slept   didn't sleep**   on mattresses.

■ C. WAS / WERE *Complete these sentences with* **was** *or* **were.**

PastTense: *be*		
I		
He	was	difficult.
She	wasn't	
It		
You	were	
We	weren't	young.
They		

1. Life __was__ very difficult for the first settlers in the New World.

2. The first homes _____ small buildings made of wood and mud.

3. There _____ no kitchen in the house.

4. There _____ no bathroom, either. There _____ a small outhouse in the back.

5. Windows _____ small, and no glass _____ available.

6. The first settlers _____ (negative) farmers or hunters, so the new settlers _____ often hungry.

7. At first, there _____ few schools in the colonies.

8. Many girls _____ married by the age of sixteen.

9. Newspapers _____ an important source of information.

10. By 1776, there _____ over two million English colonists in the New World.

■ D. PAST TENSE *Write the verb in parentheses in the past tense. Some of the verbs are irregular.*

Jamestown: The First English Settlement

In January 1607, three small ships __left__ (leave) England for America. Four months later, they _____ (arrive) in America, the New World. Several of the men on board _____ (negative—survive) the long, stormy voyage. The men _____ (choose) an area on the James River that is now in the state of Virginia. They _____ (begin) to build a fort. The men _____ (be) "gentlemen" and _____ (negative—be) used to working with their hands. Their purpose in the New World _____ (be) to hunt for gold and to start a small colony for England.

But there _____ (negative—be) any gold. The winter _____ (come) and there _____ (negative—be) enough food. Many men _____ (get) sick. By the end of the first winter, only

forty men _____ (be) still alive.

   Over the next three years, more settlers _____ (arrive), but they

_____ (negative—be) farmers, so the first few years of the colony

_____ (be) very difficult. Disease, starvation, and Indians

_____ (kill) most of the settlers. Eventually, the colonists

_____ (learn) more about farming and the weather. They

_____ (make) peace with the Indians. Tobacco, not gold,

_____ (produce) the real wealth of the new colony. Tobacco

_____ (grow) easily in the fertile soil and _____

(make) farmers out of the new settlers. As the years _____ (go) by, more

and more settlers _____ (arrive), and many small towns

_____ (grow) along the river.

> Name one historic area in your country. Why is it famous?

■ E. PAST QUESTIONS *Complete these questions about colonial times.*

Past Tense Questions			
Where			cook?
How	did	colonial people	read?
When			travel?

1. What _did the colonists grow?_____ Vegetables.

2. Where _____? In wooden houses.

3. What _____? Long dresses.

4. How _____? By horse and wagon.

5. What _____? Quill pen and ink.

6. What _____? Feather beds.

7. What _____ in the winter? Bread and meat.

8. Who _____ all the clothes? The women did.

9. What _____? Beer, cider, rum, and wine.

10. How _____? They read to one another.

> Write five questions about the story, Jamestown—The First English Settlement. Ask them to another student.

■ **F. USED TO** *Read the information about today. Then write sentences about colonial times with **used to**.*

Used to Statements		
I		write letters.
You	used to	
He		milk cows.
They		

1. Today, people eat with forks, knives, and spoons.

   People used to eat with spoons and their fingers.
   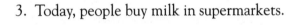

2. Today, people take many kinds of medicine.

   _____

3. Today, people buy milk in supermarkets.

   _____

herbs

4. Today, some people go to church every Sunday, but others never go.

   _____

5. Today, people buy food in supermarkets.

   _____

almost everyone

6. Today, people wear coats in the winter.

   _____

7. Today, most people cook on gas or electric stoves.

   _____

cloaks

8. Today, people drink from plastic or glass containers.

   _____

wooden mugs

26

■ A. WHAT'S WRONG WITH THIS PICTURE? *There are thirteen things wrong with this picture. In a group of four or five students, see how many you can find. Check your answers on page 35.*

EXAMPLE

Children didn't play with toy trucks.

Houses didn't have air conditioners.

B. STUDENT TO STUDENT

Student A: Read each question below and listen to **Student B** read the correct answer. Write the answers.
Student B: Turn to page 189.

1. Why didn't people travel a lot?

   _____

2. How did families who lived in different towns communicate?

   _____

3. When did newspapers become popular?

   _____

4. Who delivered the mail?

   _____

5. Who improved postal service?

   _____

When you finish number 5, change pages. **Student A** *will turn to page 189.*
Student B: Ask questions 6 to 10 and listen to **Student A** and write the answers.

6. How long did wedding celebrations last?

   _____

7. Did colonial families have pets?

   _____

8. How did neighbors help each other?

   _____

9. Where did men go to relax?

   _____

10. What kind of sports did colonial people like to watch?

   _____

■ C. INTERVIEW: CHILDHOOD

Read the list of childhood activities below. Listen to your teacher talk about his or her childhood, and check the things he or she used to do. Talk with a partner and compare your childhoods. Check what you used to do and what your partner used to do.

	Teacher	Me	Partner
1. I used to play with dolls or action figures.	❑	❑	❑
2. I used to play soccer.	❑	❑	❑
3. I used to climb trees.	❑	❑	❑
4. I used to play outside at night.	❑	❑	❑
5. I used to go to the beach.	❑	❑	❑
6. I used to draw a lot of pictures.	❑	❑	❑
7. I used to build things.	❑	❑	❑
8. I used to ride my bike.	❑	❑	❑
9. I used to get in trouble.	❑	❑	❑
10. _____	❑	❑	❑

Complete these sentences with information from the chart.

1. I used to _____.

2. I used to _____, and my partner did, too.

3. I never _____, but my partner used to.

4. My teacher used to _____, and I did, too.

5. My teacher _____, but I didn't.

Practicing on Your Own

A. PAST TENSE
Complete the sentences with the correct form of the past tense of the verbs below. Some of the sentences are negative.

be	grow	live	use	buy	have
read	wear	cook	hold	study	write

1. Colonial people __grew__ their own vegetables.

2. Colonial people _____ milk at stores.

3. Colonial people _____ on gas stoves.

4. Colonial people _____ electricity; they _____ candles.

5. Colonial people _____ letters to their friends; they _____ telephones.

6. Colonial children _____ in one-room schoolhouses; they _____ in large schools with many rooms.

7. Colonial girls _____ short skirts; they _____ long dresses and bonnets.

8. Colonial families _____ in apartments; they _____ in one- or two-story homes.

9. Colonial families _____ freedom of religion in America.

10. Colonial families _____ books to each other.

11. To make important decisions, colonial towns _____ town meetings.

12. Colonial households _____ large. Sometimes, grandparents, aunts, uncles, and cousins _____ together in one house.

B. USED TO
*Answer the questions with **used to**. Use the vocabulary to help answer the questions.*

pipes	open fires	wooden houses
wooden wheels	horses and wagons	leather boots
small brick ovens	long dresses	metal bed warmers
	salted, smoked, and dried food	

1. Did colonial people live in apartment buildings?

   No, they used to live in wooden houses.

2. Did colonial children wear sneakers?

   No, _____ .

3. Did colonial men drive cars?

   No, _____ .

4. Did colonial women bake bread in ovens?

   No, _____ .

5. Did colonial girls wear miniskirts?

   No, _____ .

6. Did colonial vehicles have tires?

   No, _____ .

7. Did colonial families use electric blankets?

   No, _____ .

8. Did colonial women cook on barbecue grills?

   No, _____ .

9. Did colonial families eat refrigerated food?

   No, _____ .

10. Did colonial men smoke cigarettes?

    No, _____ .

brick oven

metal bed warmers

■ C. USED TO *Complete these sentences about your life when you were in your country.*

1. When I lived in ___Ecuador___ , I used to ___fish___ every day.

2. When I lived in _____ , I used to _____ every day.

3. My family and I used to _____ every summer.

4. My friends and I used to _____ on Saturday nights.

5. I used to _____ television _____ hours a day.

6. I _____ typical foods such as _____ and

   _____ .

7. I _____ every morning.

8. I _____ work as a(n) _____ .

   (occupation)

9. I never used to _____ .

Plimouth Plantation

Plymouth, Massachusetts, is a popular tourist attraction. Plymouth was the site of the second colony in America. On November 11, 1620, a small ship of English settlers landed there and started a colony, looking for a better life and religious freedom.

One of the most popular attractions in Plymouth is Plimouth Plantation. Plimouth Plantation was the dream of Henry Hornblower II. When he was a boy, Hornblower read and heard stories about the pilgrims who lived in Plymouth. When he was older, he worked in Plymouth, with archaeologists. In 1945, his father gave $20,000 to the Pilgrim Society to reconstruct Plimouth Plantation. It is a replica of the original settlement, including homes, shops and gardens.

Historians studied pilgrims' journals and writings to re-create the settlement. For forty years, archaeologists studied and dug in and around the area. They found more than 350,000 artifacts from the time of the colonists. After reading many books and studying the artifacts, they made reproductions of the clothes, tools, furniture, and houses of the 1620s.

Today at Plimouth Plantation, actors wear the same kinds of clothes that the Plymouth colonists used to wear. They cook food in open fireplaces and make baskets. They use the same kinds of tools that the pilgrims used to use. When visitors talk to the "colonists," the "colonists" answer with the same English and accent that the colonists used to have. The "colonists" even raise the same types of animals and farm the same types of vegetables that were present in colonial times.

A trip to Plimouth Plantation is a trip back in history.

1. When did the pilgrims come to America?

   They came to America in 1620.
   _____

2. Was Plymouth, Massachusetts, the first colony?

   _____

3. Why did the pilgrims leave England?

   _____

4. How did Henry Hornblower II find out about the pilgrims at Plymouth?

   _____

5. Who gave a large donation to the Pilgrim Society?

   _____

6. How did the historians re-create the plantation?

   _____

7. What did archaeologists find at the plantation?

   _____

8. What do the actors wear?

   _____

9. What do the "colonists" do?

   _____

10. What language do the "colonists" speak?

    _____

Having Fun with the Language

■ **A. ROLE-PLAY** *In a group of three to five students, write ten questions you would ask the original colonists. Role-play interviews between the colonists and visitors to the colony. Half of you should be colonists. The others should be visitors and ask the questions.*

■ **B. INTERVIEW** *Interview a person who is sixty years old or older. Your teacher might be able to ask an older friend or relative to visit the class. Before the visitor arrives, develop a list of questions about life fifty years ago. Ask about transportation, television, the movies, the telephone, shopping malls, entertainment, and the cost of items such as a soda, gas, or a postage stamp. After your guest leaves, write a short paragraph comparing life fifty years ago and life today.*

■ **C. A LETTER TO ENGLAND** *Choose one of the following roles:*

   a. a thirty-year-old single man
   b. a forty-year-old married man or woman with a family
   c. a sixteen-year-old single girl who lives with her parents
   d. a ten-year-old boy or girl

You are living at Plimouth Plantation. Write a letter back to your relatives in England. Talk about your life in the New World. Describe your town, your house, your neighbors, and what you do for fun. Read your letter to a group of your classmates.

Grammar Summary

■ **I. Past tense**

We use the past tense to talk about actions that happened in the past time.

Regular past verbs end with **ed.**

The chart of irregular past verbs is on page 187 in the Appendix.

■ **2. Past time expressions**

yesterday	a few minutes ago	last night	in 1750
the day before yesterday	a few days ago	last week	in 1962
	a few weeks ago	last year	

■ 3. Past tense: *be*

Jamestown **was** the first English settlement.

Many settlers **were** very religious.

Was the voyage long and difficult?	Yes, it **was.**
Were the settlers farmers?	No, they **weren't.**
Where was the first settlement?	It **was** in Jamestown.

■ 4. Past tense

Regular verbs	**Irregular verbs**
Colonial people **worked** hard.	Colonial women **wore** long dresses.
They **lived** on farms.	Colonial families **had** gardens.
Families **didn't live** in cities.	Houses **didn't have** bathrooms.
Did children **attend** school?	**Did** children **wear** sneakers?
Yes, they **did.**	No, they **didn't.**
Where **did** colonial people **live**?	When **did** the first colonies **begin**?
They **lived** on farms.	They **began** in the 1600s.

■ 5. *Used to*

Used to shows habitual or repeated action in the past. The action was true in the past, but not any longer.

People **used to milk** their own cows.	(Now people buy milk in the supermarket.)
I **used to live** near the beach.	(Now I live in the city.)

Answers to A. Working Together, page 27

Note: Be sure you have the same ideas. Your sentences may be different!

1. Children didn't play with toy trucks.
2. Houses didn't have air conditioners.
3. People didn't fly helicopters.
4. People didn't smoke cigarettes.
5. Girls didn't wear short skirts. (mini-skirts)
6. People didn't wear sneakers.
7. Wagons didn't have rubber tires.
8. Farmers didn't use tractors.
9. Streets didn't have traffic lights.
10. Towns did not have paved streets.
11. Women didn't cook on barbecue grills.
12. People didn't have electricity.
13. People didn't have portable tape players.

Future: *be + going to* and *will*

Grammar in Action

GOING TO

▪▪

A. LISTEN: THE DIVORCE *Look at the pictures and listen to the story of Tom and Amy's divorce.*

Vocabulary
alimony   child support   joint custody

*Complete the sentences below with **be + going to** and the verb in parentheses. Some of the statements are negative.*

Future: *be + going to*			
I	am		move.
	am not		
He	is	going to	get a divorce.
	isn't		
They	are		stay home.
	aren't		

1. Tom and Amy _are going to get_ (get) a divorce.

2. Tom _____ (leave) this weekend.

3. He _____ (live) in the same town.

4. The children _____ (be) upset.

5. Amy _____ (keep) the house.

6. The children _____ (go) to a different school.

7. Carly and Jason _____ (be) with their father on the weekends.

8. Tom _____ (pay) alimony.

7. Amy _____ (stay) home during the day anymore.

8. She _____ (look) for a job.

■ **B. ANYMORE** *Life is going to be very different for the Larson family. Change these sentences to the future negative and use **anymore**.*

> **EXAMPLE**
>
> Amy is a full-time homemaker.
> She **isn't going to be** a full-time homemaker **anymore**.

1. Tom comes home for dinner.
2. The family eats dinner together.
3. The children see their father every day.
4. Their father reads to them every night.
5. The family takes a vacation together in the summer.
6. Tom comes home to his family after work.
7. Amy stays home all day.
8. Amy is home when the children get home from school.

```
How else is life going to change for
Tom and Amy and the children?
```

■ C. QUESTIONS *Answer these questions about Tom and Amy's divorce.*

Future Questions				
When	is	he		
Where	are	you	going to	move?
Why	are	they		

1. When were Tom and Amy married?
2. How long were they married?
3. Did they try to work out their problems?
4. When is Tom going to leave?
5. Where is he going to move?
6. How many children do they have?
7. Who are the children going to live with during the week?
8. Who are they going to live with on the weekends?
9. What are they going to do in the summer?
10. How long is Tom going to pay alimony?
11. What is going to happen after seven years?
12. Did Amy work before this?
13. Is she going to need to look for a job?
14. Is she going to study part time or full time?

■ D. PRESENT CONTINUOUS FOR FUTURE *Tom is going to move soon. Use these cues to describe his future plans in the present continuous tense.*

> **Present Continuous: Future Meaning**
> If a specific time in the future is stated or understood,
> the present continuous can show future meaning.

EXAMPLE

move/ tomorrow　　　He is moving tomorrow.

1. pack / tonight
2. rent a van / this weekend
3. move / on Sunday
4. his brother / help / him move
5. sign a lease / for a year
6. take / his stereo system
7. buy / a new TV / next week
8. buy / new furniture / next month
9. telephone company / install his phone / on Monday
10. see / his lawyer / next week

> What are your plans for tomorrow?
> Use the present continuous.

WILL

A. WILL *Complete these sentence about Amy's plans. Use* **will** *or* **won't** *and an appropriate verb.*

need	study	help
attend	cover	receive
hire	look	stay

Future: *will*

I	will	move.
She	won't	stay home.
They		

1. Amy __will look_____ for a job.

2. Amy _____ school part time.

3. She _____ accounting.

4. She _____ home all day anymore.

5. Amy _____ medical benefits from Tom's employer for one year. After

   that, his company _____ only the children.

6. Amy _____ a baby sitter for the children in the afternoon.

7. Amy's mother _____ her if the children are sick.

8. Amy _____ a lawyer to help her with the divorce agreement.

B. OFFERS TO HELP *You are a helpful person. Offer to help each person below. Use the expressions in the box to help you.*

EXAMPLE

Who will drive my children to school if it's raining?
Don't worry. I'll drive them.

1. I don't understand the homework.
2. My car broke down and I don't have a ride to school.
3. I can't find my keys.
4. I don't know how to program my VCR.
5. I just moved in and I don't know anybody around here.
6. How do you get to Springfield?
7. I wrote this report, but I need some one to read it over for me.
8. My bicycle has a flat tire.
9. I received a letter in English, but I don't understand it.
10. My income taxes are due, but I don't know how to fill out the form.

Vocabulary

help you
introduce you
give you directions
help you find them
show you how
translate it
check it
change it
give you a ride

C. PREDICTIONS *Sit in a small group. Read these predictions about the future of the family in the next twenty years. Check* **Agree** *or* **Disagree**. *Explain the reason for your choice.*

	Agree	Disagree
1. Families will have more children.	❏	❏
2. The number of divorces will increase.	❏	❏
3. There will be more single mothers.	❏	❏
4. More women will stay home and take care of their children.	❏	❏
5. More people will work from home offices.	❏	❏
6. More men will stay home with their children.	❏	❏
7. Men will help more with household chores.	❏	❏
8. Women will receive the same pay as men.	❏	❏
9. More companies will offer day care facilities.	❏	❏
10. More grandparents will live with their children.	❏	❏

> What is one change that is going to take place in your life in the next year or two? How will your life change?

Future Time Clauses

A. FUTURE PLANS *Sonia, a young college student, is dreaming about her future. Match these sentence halves which tell about her plans.*

Future Time Clause	
Time clause	**Main clause**
If I study hard,	I'll graduate in two more years.

_____ 1. After she saves some money,   a. she'll get a promotion

_____ 2. If she meets the right person,   b. she'll buy a new car.

_____ 3. If she works hard,   c. she'll travel around Europe.

_____ 4. When she takes a vacation,   d. she'll get married.

Now, use your imagination and continue to write about Sonia's future. Each sentence begins with a time clause. The main clause takes the future tense.

1. Before Sonia gets married, _____.

2. When she has children, _____.

3. If she decides to become a full-time mother, _____ .

4. If she has a lot of children, _____ .

5. After her children are grown, _____ .

6. If Sonia decides to change careers, _____ .

7. When Sonia has enough money, _____ .

8. When Sonia retires, _____ .

■ B. A HAPPY LIFE
George is 20 years old. Sit with a partner, talk about his life, and put these important events in an order that you both like. Number the events from 1 to 8. Talk about the events using **before** *or* **after.**

> **EXAMPLE**
>
> Before George **finds** a job, he's **going to graduate** from college.
> After he **meets** a wonderful woman, he's **going to ge**t married.

find a good job	have a daughter
buy a house	have a son
get married	meet a wonderful woman
1. graduate from college	save a lot of money

■ C. MAYBE TOMORROW...
Answer each **When** *question with a sentence containing a future time clause. Use* **after, before, if,** *or* **when.**

> **EXAMPLE**
>
> When are you going to get married?
> I'm going to get married when I find the perfect man.

1. When are you going to get married?
2. When are you going to graduate from college?
3. When are you going to look for a different job?
4. When are you going to do your homework?
5. When are you going to call your parents?
6. When are you going to pay the telephone bill?
7. When are you going to travel out of the country?
8. When are you going to start to exercise?
9. When are you going to buy a new car?
10. When are you going to give a party?

Working Together

■ A. THE DIVORCE AGREEMENT
In a small group, decide on a divorce agreement between Tom and Amy. The box shows Tom and Amy's assets. Decide on the specifics, answering the questions below.

Tom and Amy Larson	
Tom's salary:	$42,000 a year ($3,500 a month)
Savings:	$10,000 in the bank
House:	The house is worth $100,000 The house has a $50,000 mortgage
Cars:	1995 Toyota, 1997 Ford Taurus
Pension:	$30,000
Furniture:	Household furniture
Electronics:	TV, VCR, stereo, computer

1. How much money is Tom going to pay in child support?
   How much alimony is he going to pay?
   How much is he going to keep for himself?
2. How will Tom and Amy divide their savings?
3. Who is going to keep the house? Who is going to pay the mortgage and taxes?
4. Who will get each car?
5. How are they going to divide Tom's pension?
6. Who will keep the furniture?
7. Who will keep the electronic equipment?
8. Who is going to pay for college for Jason and Carly?

■ B. CHANGES
How will life change for each of these people? List four changes that will occur for each person or couple.

> Make two predictions about the future of the family in your country.

C. FIND SOMEONE WHO *Walk around the room and ask your classmates these questions about their future plans. Use* **be + going to** *or* **will.** *Try to find someone who answers* **Yes** *to each item. Write that student's name on the line.*

Are you going to change jobs?   No, I'm not. (Continue to ask other students.)

Are you going to change jobs?   Yes, I am. (Write that student's name.)

1. get married?   _____

2. move?   _____

3. visit your native country?   _____

4. buy a house?   _____

5. see a lawyer?   _____

6. go to a wedding?   _____

7. change jobs?   _____

8. take a vacation?   _____

9. start a business?   _____

10. graduate from college?   _____

D. STUDENT TO STUDENT *You each have a short sentence.* **Student A** *will read his or her sentence, and then* **Student B** *will read his or her sentence for the same number. Combine the sentences with a future time clause using* **before** *or* **after.** *Write the five new sentences below. Remember to use pronouns for repeated names.*

Student A: *Look at page 190.*
Student B: *Look at page 192.*

1. _____

2. _____

3. _____

4. _____

5. _____

Practicing on Your Own

■ A. FUTURE *Complete these sentences with the verb in the future tense. Use the be + going to or will form.*

1. The children _are going to feel_ (feel) upset when their parents split up.

2. Carly _____ (talk) with her teacher.

3. Tom and Amy _____ (try) to communicate with one another.

4. The children _____ (stay) in the same house.

5. They _____ (keep) their friends.

6. Carly and Jason _____ (walk) home after school together.

7. They _____ (have) a baby sitter in the afternoon.

8. Carly and Jason _____ (stay) with their father on the weekends.

9. Tom _____ still _____ (coach) Jason's soccer team.

10. Tom _____ (take) Carly to her trumpet lessons on Fridays.

■ B. CONVERSATION *Complete this conversation between Tom and the children. Use the present or future tense.*

Tom: Kids, don't worry. I _am going to be_ in the next town.
                                    (be)

Carly: But Daddy, why _____ you _____ us?
                                                                              (leave)

Tom: It's hard to explain. Mommy and I both _____ you, but we
                                                                    (love)

_____ each other anymore. We _____ friends, but
(love—negative)   (be)

we _____ married.
      (stay—negative)

Jason: But, Dad, we _____ you to stay here.
                                      (want)

44

Tom: I know, but I _____ far. And you _____
    (be—negative)   (live)

with me on the weekends.

Carly: Dad, you always _____ me a story at night. Who
                              read)

_____ me a story before I _____ to bed?
    (read)   (go)

Tom: Mommy _____ you a story. And I _____
                    (read)   (read)

to you on the weekends. Remember, when you _____ school on
                                               (leave)

Friday, you _____ to my apartment.
               (come)

Carly: I _____ you to leave, Daddy.
              (want—negative)

Tom: I _____ to leave you, either, Carly. It _____
            (want—negative)   (be—negative)

easy, but everything _____ out.
                         (work)

■ C. SENTENCE COMBINING *The students in one ESL class gave these "hints" for a happy marriage. Combine their sentences using the word in parentheses and a future time clause.*

1. I'm going to get married. I'm going to meet the right person. (when)
2. We're going to get married. My husband and I are going to have credit in our own names. (after)
3. I'm going to feel tired. My husband is going to cook dinner. (when)
4. I'm going to be busy. My wife is going to cut the lawn. (if)
5. We are going to have an argument. The whole family isn't going to know about it. (if)
6. My mother will come for a visit. She will only stay for a week. (when)
7. My husband is going to tell me something in confidence. I'm going to keep it to myself. (when)
8. My husband is going to tell the same joke twice. I'm still going to laugh. (if)
9. We are going to go to bed each night. I'm going to tell my husband I love him. (before)
10. I'm going to get home from work. I'm going to tell my wife that she's beautiful. (after)

Sharing our Stories

 This couple is going to get a divorce after five years of marriage. They don't have any children. They have a house and two cars, a cat and a dog and a houseful of furniture. They both work and have similar salaries.

Sit with another student and name the man and the woman. Write a conversation between them. How are they going to divide their assets?

Sit with another group of two students. Read your conversations.

Having Fun With the Language

■ **A. THE CAUSES OF DIVORCE** In the United States, 50 percent of all marriages end in divorce. In a group, decide on five major causes of divorce.

■ **B. FAMILIES** A traditional family used to be a mother and father with one or more children. The mother usually stayed home and the father worked. Today, the word "family" has taken on a new meaning, and there are many kinds of loving family arrangements. Add to this list of families and family arrangements:

1. The mother and father work and the children have a baby sitter.
2. The mother and father are divorced. The children live with one parent.
3. The mother and father are divorced. The children live with one parent and one stepparent.
4. The children live with their grandparents or other relatives.
5. _____
6. _____
7. _____

46

Grammar Summary

■ 1. The future tense

We use the future tense to talk about actions in the future time, such as tomorrow, next week, next year, etc. There are two forms of the future, **be + going to** and **will.**

Both future forms talk about future actions and plans.

In addition, *will* expresses promises or predictions.

■ 2. Present continuous tense: future meaning

If a specific time in the future is stated or understood, the present continuous can show future meaning.

Tom is leaving this weekend.

He's taking the kids on vacation in July.

■ 3. Future time expressions

tomorrow	in a few minutes	soon
the day after tomorrow	in an hour	later
next week	in a little while	
next year		

■ 4. Future: *be + going to*   Future: *will*

I'm going to move soon.	I will move next month.
She's going to get a divorce.	She will get a divorce.
Are you going to move?	Will you move?
Is Tom going to pay alimony?	Will Tom pay alimony?
When are you going to move?	When will you move?
Where is Tom going to live?	Where will Tom live?

■ 5. Future time clauses

Many sentences contain time clauses. A time clause begins with word such as *if, when, before, after,* and *as soon as.* A time clause has a subject and a verb, but it is not a complete sentence by itself. A time clause may come at the beginning or the end of a sentence. With a future time clause, the verb in the main clause is in the **future tense.** The verb in the time clause is in the **present tense.**

I'll get married **when I meet the right person.**

When I meet the right person, I'll get married.*

*Note: When a time clause comes at the beginning of a sentence, use a comma to separate it from the main clause.

■ 6. Pronunciation

Going to is usually pronounced **gonna.**

Tom and Amy are going to get a divorce.

Tom and Amy are gonna* get a divorce.

*Note: **gonna** is only a spoken form. Do not use **gonna** when you are writing.

4 The Apartment

Comparative and Superlative Adjectives

A. LISTEN: ALI'S NEIGHBORHOOD

Ali lives in an apartment in this neighborhood. The neighborhood has changed a lot in the past five years, and he wants to move. Listen to his story and fill in the chart with the adjectives in the box. You can use two adjectives to describe some of the problems.

clean—dirty   quiet—noisy

nice—not nice   convenient—inconvenient

safe—dangerous   cheap—expensive

friendly—unfriendly   helpful—not helpful

	Five Years Ago	Today
The neighborhood		
The neighbors		
The stores and groceries		
The streets and sidewalks		
The superintendent	Mr. Morales	Mr. Johnson

■ B. COMPARATIVE ADJECTIVE FORM *Write the comparative form of these adjectives.*

Irregular Comparatives
good—better
bad—worse

One syllable	Two syllables, ending with *y:*	Two or more syllables, not ending with *y:*
large—larger than	busy—busier than	modern—more modern than
old—older than	pretty—prettier than	dangerous—more dangerous than
big—bigger than	ugly—uglier than	convenient—more convenient than

attractive *more attractive than*   convenient _____

safe *safer than*   cheap _____

dangerous _____   friendly _____

quiet _____   nice _____

expensive _____   helpful _____

dirty _____   noisy _____

■ C. COMPARATIVES *Complete these sentences about Ali's neighborhood with a comparative adjective from the list above.*

1. Five years ago, Ali's neighborhood was _more attractive than_____ it is today.

2. There's a lot of crime in Ali's neighborhood now. Five years ago, Ali's neighborhood was

   _____ it is today.

3. Five years ago, Ali's neighbors were _____ his neighbors are today.

   They were also _____ his neighbors are today.

4. The neighborhood was _____ it is today; there were more stores, and

   they were _____ the stores that are there now.

5. The streets and sidewalks are _____ they used to be five years ago.

6. The superintendent, Mr. Morales, was _____ Mr. Johnson, the current

   superintendent. Mr. Morales was also _____ Mr. Johnson.

■ D. NEIGHBORHOOD COMPARISON

Ali's friends, the Silvas, live in the same city, but in a different neighborhood. Read the two sentences and compare the neighborhoods, using the adjective in parentheses.

EXAMPLE

Statement: The Silvas' neighborhood doesn't have any garbage on the street. Ali's neighborhood has a lot of garbage on the street. (clean)

Comparison: The Silvas' neighborhood **is cleaner than** Ali's.

1. There are three groceries, two laundromats, and many other stores in the Silvas' neighborhood. There are only two stores in Ali's neighborhood. (convenient)

2. The Silvas' neighborhood has clean streets and many trees. Ali's neighborhood has dirty streets and few trees. (attractive)

3. There are many crimes in Ali's neighborhood. There are few crimes in the Silvas' neighborhood. (dangerous)

4. Ali's building is sixty-three years old. The Silvas' building is ten years old. (old)

5. Ali's building is four stories high. The Silvas' building is fifteen stories high. (tall)

6. The Silvas' building has a doorman and a video screen. Ali's building has an intercom. (safe)

7. The Silva's building is thirty minutes from their jobs. Ali's building is only ten minutes from his job. (convenient)

8. Ali's rent is $500 a month. The Silvas' rent is $700 a month. (cheap)

9. The Silvas' apartment has four rooms. Ali's apartment has two rooms. (large)

10. The Silvas' superintendent takes care of all problems right away. Ali can never find his superintendent when he needs him. (efficient)

■ E. SUPERLATIVE ADJECTIVE FORM *Write the superlative form of these adjectives.*

One syllable	Two syllables, ending with *y:*	Two or more syllables, not ending with *y:*
tall—the tallest	noisy—the noisiest	economical—the most economical
safe—the safest	pretty—the prettiest	dangerous—the most dangerous
big —the biggest	dirty—the dirtiest	convenient—the most convenient

new	the newest	expensive	_____
helpful	the most helpful	dark	_____
sunny	_____	good	_____
bright	_____	ugly	_____
friendly	_____	old	_____
sunny	_____	small	_____
spacious	_____	beautiful	_____

> **Irregular Superlatives**
> good—better—best
> bad—worse—worst

■ F. THREE APARTMENTS *The chart gives information about three apartments in the same city: Ali's, the Silvas', and Linda's apartments. Use superlative adjectives from exercise E and form sentences comparing the apartments.*

EXAMPLE

Ali's apartment is **the oldest**.

The Silvas' apartment is **the most expensive**.

Ali's apartment is **the least expensive**.

	Ali's	The Silvas'	Linda's*
Age of building	63	10	20
Rent	$500	$700	$600
Size	2 rooms	4 rooms	5 rooms
Light	sunny	very sunny	dark
Neighbors	not friendly	friendly	very friendly
Kitchen	tiny	medium-sized	large
Superintendent	not helpful	helpful	very helpful
View	ugly	beautiful	nice

* Ali's girlfriend

■ G. SUPERLATIVES *Answer the questions about the three apartments.*

Whose apartment is the oldest?   Ali's is.

1. Whose apartment is the newest?

2. Whose apartment is the most expensive? The least expensive?

3. Whose apartment is the smallest? The largest?

4. Whose apartment is the brightest? The darkest?

5. Whose neighbors are the friendliest?

6. Whose kitchen is the least spacious?

7. Whose view is the best?

8. Whose superintendent is the least helpful?

9. Whose superintendent is the most helpful?

H. LISTEN: *As...as* *Listen to the information about two groceries in Ali's neighborhood. Fill in the missing adjective forms with* **(not) as** _____ **as.** *Check your answers on page 59.*

(fresh) The vegetables at the Green Market are **as fresh as** the vegetables at the International Market. *Note: They're the same; they both have fresh vegetables.*

(high) The International Market's prices are **not as high as** the Green Market's prices. *Note: The Green Market is more expensive.*

1. (juicy) The Green Market's oranges are _____

   the International Market's.

2. (delicious) The Green Market's meat is _____

   the International Market's.

3. (crowded) The Green Market's shelves are _____

   the International Market's.

4. (large) The selection at the Green Market is _____

   the International Market's.

5. (courteous) The cashiers at the International Market are _____

   _____ the cashiers at the Green Market.

6. (helpful) The manager at the International Market is _____

   _____ the manager at the Green Market.

7. (quick) The delivery service at the International Market is _____

   _____ the Green Market's.

8. (high) The prices at the International Market are _____

   _____ the prices at the Green Market.

Working Together

■ A. OUR APARTMENTS *Sit in a group of three students and complete this chart about your apartments.*

	Student 1	Student 2	Student 3
Rent (high, medium, low)			
Number of rooms			
Size of kitchen			
Neighbors (friendly, unfriendly)			
Noise (quiet, noisy)			
View (nice, ugly, beautiful)			
Superintendent			
Distance from school	____ minutes from school	____ minutes from school	____ minutes from school

Together, write ten sentences comparing your apartments and neighborhoods. Use comparative and

*superlative adjectives and **as** _____ **as**.*

■ B. THE BEST AND THE WORST
In a group of three or four students, decide on a person or place in your city for each of the following. Use the superlative form of the expression.

| interesting bookstore | → | **The most interesting** bookstore in this city is the Book Bag. |
| delicious pastries | → | We can buy **the most delicious** pastries at the French Bakery. |

1. good coffee
2. bad coffee
3. delicious bread
4. boring place
5. busy street

6. fashionable place to shop
7. crowded place
8. good place to meet people
9. important person
10. relaxing spot

> Write one more sentence about your city or area, using the superlative.

■ C. CLASSIFIED ADS
Three roommates are looking for an apartment to rent. Read the following classified ads. Complete the abbreviation chart. Decide which apartment your group likes the best.

2 BR apt, only min from town, close to shopping; near bus. New kitchen and appliances, new thermal windows. Off-street parking, 24-hr security. No pets. 1 mo security. $525. See super 486-7601.

2 BR apt in 2-family, historic bldg, 30 min from downtown, near subway, shopping and elem school. Quiet, ethnic neighborhood. Efficiency kitchen, hdwd floors, laundry in basement. Pets OK. 1 1/2 mo security. $850. Call owner. 476-9366.

2 BR apt, $675, util incl. Downtown, 1 block to bus & subway, on-street parking. Intercom. Sunny. New refrig & stove. Pets OK. Avail immed. Please call 476-3971.

Abbreviations

apt	apartment
avail	
bldg	
BR	
elem	
hdwd	
hr	
immed	
incl	
min	
mo	
refrig	
super	
util	

■ D. DISCUSSION
Discuss the following questions in a small group.

1. Where do you live now, in an apartment or in a house? Describe it.
2. What do you like about it? What don't you like?
3. Do you like your neighborhood? Why or why not?
4. How does your home in the United States compare with your home in your country?
5. Do you want to move? Why or why not?

■ A. ADJECTIVES—CONTRAST

	Rich and Jane	Steve	Susan
Age of building	5 years	60 years	20 years
Rent	$800 a month	$500 a month	$800 a month
Number of floors	15	4	10
Number of rooms	4	3	3
Convenience	not convenient	very convenient	convenient
Neighbors	not friendly	very friendly	friendly
Superintendent	helpful	not helpful	very helpful

Circle the correct adjective according to the apartment information in the chart.

1. Rich and Jane's apartment is   **older than**   **not as old as**   Susan's.

2. Steve's building is   **the oldest**   **the newest.**

3. Susan's apartment is   **more expensive than**   **as expensive as**   Rich and Jane's.

4. Steve's apartment is   **the most expensive**   **the cheapest.**

5. Rich and Jane's building is   **taller than**   **as tall as**   Steve's.

6. Susan's apartment is   **not as big as**   **as big as**   Steve's.

7. Steve's apartment is   **the least convenient**   **the most convenient.**

Complete these sentences according to the apartment information in the chart.

8. Susan's apartment is _____ Richard and Jane's. (convenient)

9. Rich and Jane's neighbors are _____ Steve's. (friendly)

10. Susan's neighbors are _____ Steve's. (friendly)

11. Steve's superintendent is _____ of the three. (helpful)

12. Steve's rent is _____ than Susan's. (low)

13. Steve's rent is _____ of all. (low)

14. I think _____'s apartment is _____ of the three.

    (good)

■ B. MY OLD NEIGHBORHOOD

Using the adjectives below, write eight sentences comparing the neighborhood where you grew up and the neighborhood where you live now. Write four sentences using comparative adjectives and four with (not) as _____ as.

> ### EXAMPLE
>
> (nice) The neighborhood where I grew up was **nicer** than Riverside.   *or*
>   The neighborhood where I grew up was **as nice as** Riverside.

  1. quiet   2. noisy   3. crowded   4. safe   5. friendly   6. helpful

Write two more sentences comparing the neighborhoods.

■ C. STORY

Read this story. Use the cues and ask and answer the questions below.

a ranch

a split level

a Victorian

Jane and Rich are expecting a baby soon. Right now they're living in a one-bedroom apartment. They've decided to move into a house so that they'll have more room. They think a one-bedroom apartment will be too small for them after the baby is born. Rich's mother is a real estate agent, so she's helping them find a house. So far, they've seen three houses, but they can't decide which one to buy.

First, Jane and Rich looked at a twelve-year-old ranch-style house on Smith Street. It is only twenty minutes from their offices. It has two bedrooms, a living room, a dining room, a kitchen, a bathroom, and a large unfinished basement. Jane likes it because it has a fireplace and a large back yard. Rich isn't sure about it. It doesn't have much closet space, and he would like to have a third bedroom to use as an office. The house is in a nice neighborhood, but the schools aren't very good. It has a detached one-car garage, but it has a long driveway, so they could park the second car in the driveway. The asking price is $110,000.

Next, they looked at a small ten-year-old split-level house on Hope Street. That house is ten minutes from their offices. It also has two bedrooms, a living room, and a dining room, and it has a large kitchen. There is a lot of closet space. There is one full bathroom upstairs and a powder room on the first floor. It has a basement, but it will need a lot of work before it is usable. The back yard is very small, so they won't be able to put in a pool. Rich likes the house because the garage is attached. Rich won't have to worry about mowing a big lawn because it has a small front lawn. The neighborhood is okay on that block, but three blocks away there is a lot of crime. The asking price is $70,000.

Finally, Rich's mother showed them a beautiful Victorian house on Brook Street. It is eighty years old. The house is forty-five minutes from their offices in a very nice neighborhood. The house needs painting, new plumbing, and a new roof, but it has three bedrooms, a living room with fireplace, a dining room, a very large kitchen with a pantry, and a deck. There are two bathrooms and a lot of closet space. The back yard is big enough for a pool, and there is also a large front lawn. There is a two-car garage in the back. There are many excellent schools in the area. The asking price is $170,000. Both Jane and Rich love the house, but they think it is too expensive for them.

1. Which house / big?

   _Which house is the biggest?_____   _The Victorian house is._____

2. Which house / expensive?

   _____ ? _____ .

3. Which house / modern?

   _____ ? _____ .

4. Which house / in a good neighborhood?

   _____ ? _____ .

5. Which house / close to their jobs?

   _____ ? _____ .

6. Which house / in good condition?

   _____ ? _____ .

7. Which house / spacious?

   _____ ? _____ .

8. Which house has / convenient parking?

   _____ ? _____ .

Which house should they buy? Explain your answer.

_____

_____

_____

Sharing Our Stories

Read Thien's story about his home in Vietnam and his home here.

My family is from Da Nang, a large city in the southern part of Vietnam. Our home there was about ten minutes from the ocean. Vietnam is a tropical country and the homes help you feel cooler. Most homes in Vietnam are one floor and are made of cement. The doors and windows are large with no glass or screens so that the breeze can flow through. The rooms where people talk and sit and eat are large, comfortable, and airy. The bedrooms are smaller and less important. Typically, the children in the family sleep in one bedroom on the floor on thin mattresses with mosquito netting.

My two older brothers came to the United States many years ago. They saved and planned. They tried for many years to receive permission for our family to leave Vietnam. Finally, in 1993, my mother and father, four more brothers, and my sister were allowed to leave Vietnam. My brothers bought this house for us in the suburbs in New Jersey! It's a beautiful old house and is very different for us. It is made of wood and has many windows and doors, but they are small and have storm windows. It's very cold for us and in the winter, the house feels closed. There are many large bedrooms. In the United States, the bedrooms have beds and a lot of furniture. People spend a lot of time in their bedrooms, studying, reading, or listening to music. My mother enjoys the modern kitchen with appliances she can depend on. In Vietnam, we had to go shopping every day. We couldn't depend on a steady flow of electricity for refrigerators, stoves, and dishwashers. And the bathrooms in the United States are in the house, which is much more convenient! We like our home here, but we also miss our home in Vietnam.

—Thien Le, Vietnam

Write about your home in your native country and/or your home in the United States. Describe the location, structure, rooms, and other features. Add details that will help the other students to picture your home in their minds as they read your description.

58

A. IN TOWN *With a group of your classmates, name the following in your town, and then report your choices to your other classmates.*

the oldest building   the noisiest street   the busiest intersection
the tallest building   the most beautiful house of worship   the most interesting place
the biggest park   the most important city building

B. LIBRARY ASSIGNMENT *Visit your public library and locate* The Guinness Book of World Records. *Copy eight to ten interesting or unusual facts. Share your information with four or five other students.*

C. CLASSIFIED ADS *Bring in the classified ad section of your local newspaper. What kind of apartments are available? Do you think the prices are high or reasonable? What is the most expensive area to live in? What is the safest area to live in?*

Grammar Summary

1. Comparative adjectives

The comparative form of the adjective compares two people or things.
Ali's apartment is **older than** the Silvas' apartment.
Ali's neighborhood is **more dangerous than** the Silvas' neighborhood.

2. Superlative adjectives

The superlative form of the adjective compares three or more people or things.
Ali's apartment is **the oldest.**
Ali's neighborhood is **the most dangerous.**

3. Irregular adjectives

	Irregulars	
good	better than	the best
bad	worse than	the worst
far	farther than	the farthest
	more than	the most
	less	the least

4. *As* _____ *as*

We use **as** _____ **as** to compare two people or things.
Ali's rent is **as high as** Mary's rent.   (Their rent is the same.)
Ali's rent is**n't as high as** Mary's rent.   (Mary's rent is higher.)

Answers for Exercise H (pp. 52–53)

1. as juicy as
2. as delicious as
3. not as crowded as
4. not as large as
5. as courteous as
6. as helpful as
7. not as quick as
8. not as high as

5 A Vacation to Canada

Question Review

Grammar in Action

 A. LISTEN: THE YANG FAMILY *You're going to hear a story about the Yang family. Listen and take notes about their ages, jobs, places of work or school, and interests.*

B. LISTEN *Now listen again and check your notes. Then listen to each question and circle the correct answer.*

1. a. 36.   b. 46.   c. 40.
2. a. He's 17.   b. He's 19.   c. He's 29.
3. a. Thailand.   b. Taiwan.   c. Hong Kong.
4. a. Last year.   b. Three years ago.   c. Three months ago.
5. a. Yes, they did.   b. No, they didn't.   c. Only William did.
6. a. At a college.   b. At a hospital.   c. At an office.
7. a. He's a nurse.   b. He's a doctor.   c. He's an accountant.
8. a. She's a nurse.   b. She's a teacher.   c. She's a doctor.
9. a. They work.   b. Every day.   c. They're students.
10. a. Yes, he is.   b. No, he isn't.   c. Yes, he was.
11. a. Yes, she is.   b. She volunteers.   c. She's 67.
12. a. To Montreal.   b. To Vancouver.   c. In San Francisco.

> Listen again and write each question.

C. YES/NO QUESTIONS *The Yangs are going to visit their relatives in Vancouver, Canada. Read each fact about Vancouver. Then make each statement into a **Yes/No** question and ask a classmate the question. Finally, guess whether the fact is true or false. Check your answers on page 74.*

EXAMPLE

Vancouver is in British Columbia.

Is Vancouver in British Columbia?   *Yes, it is. (True)*

1. Vancouver is in southwestern Canada.
2. The population is 350,000.
3. Twenty-five percent of the population is South American.
4. Vancouver has a mild climate.
5. Vancouver has mountains or water on all sides.
6. It is one of Canada's smallest industrial centers.
7. There are beautiful gardens in Vancouver.
8. The 1986 World's Fair was in Vancouver.
9. Vancouver's Chinatown is the largest in North America.

Be: yes/no questions		
Is	he	
Was	it	in Canada?
Are	they	
Were		

Present tense: yes/no questions			
Do	you	live	in Canada?
	they		
Does	he		

◼ D. WHO/WHOM/WHOSE QUESTIONS *Circle the correct question word. Then write the*
short answer.

Whose, Who, and Whom	
Whose	umbrella is under the chair?
Who	has two children?
	came late today?
Whom	are you going to go to the movies with?
Who	did you call last night?

Whose refers to possession.

Who refers to the object.

Whom and **who** can refer to the subject.   **Whom** is more formal.

1. **Who   Whom   Whose**   has a bilingual dictionary? _____ does.

2. **Who   Whom   Whose**   book is that? It's _____'s.

3. **Who   Whom   Whose**   do you sit next to? _____ .

4. **Who   Whom   Whose**   comes with you to class? _____ does.

5. **Who   Whom   Whose**   did you telephone last week? _____ .

6. **Who   Whom   Whose**   picture is in your wallet? _____'s.

7. **Who   Whom   Whose**   music do you like? _____'s.

8. **Who   Whom   Whose**   did you talk to before class? _____ .

9. **Who   Whom   Whose**   does the cooking at your house? _____ do / does.

10. **Who   Whom   Whose**   is wearing jeans today? _____ is.

*Work with a partner. Take turns asking and answering the questions above with a classmate's name.
Now write three more questions about your class. Ask a different classmate your questions.*

11. Who _____?

12. Whom _____?

13. Whose _____?

■ E. HOW QUESTIONS Complete these questions with the correct How expression. Then answer the question.

How questions		
How often do you come to school?	Once a week.	Every day.
How much money do you have?	$5.00.	A lot.
How many do you have?	Six.	Just one.
How long did you wait?	Ten minutes.	Three years.
How do you get to work?	By train.	I drive.
How far is it to Montreal?	100 miles.	Six hours.

1. _How often_____ do you visit your native country?

2. _____ siblings do you have?

3. _____ do you spend on transportation to school?

4. _____ are you going to stay in this country?

5. _____ hours do you sleep a night?

6. _____ do you get to school?

7. _____ do you go to the movies?

8. _____ did it take you to get to class today?

9. _____ is it from your home to school?

Now listen to your teacher read the questions and check your answers.

■ F. MIXED QUESTIONS Form questions with these cues. Then take turns asking your teacher each question.

1. where / you / grow up?
2. how many siblings / you / have?
3. what / you / want to be / when you were a child?
4. you/ speak / another language?
5. how many languages / you / speak?
6. when/ you / start to teach at this school?
7. what kind of music / you / like?
8. who / your favorite musician?
9. you / going to take / a vacation / next summer?

Wh questions
What **is** your address?
When **does** class **begin**?
Where **did** you **buy** that CD?

G. LISTEN: TAG QUESTIONS Listen and draw an arrow showing the correct
intonation. Circle the verbs.

EXAMPLE

The Yangs are going to Canada, aren't they? ⬂   falling intonation ⬂
(The speaker expects a "yes" answer.)

You weren't born in Canada, were you? ⬈   rising intonation ⬈
(The speaker isn't sure of the answer.)

1. The Yangs (live) in San Francisco, don't they? ⬂

2. Canada has two official languages, doesn't it?

3. Canada was first settled by the French, wasn't it?

4. Americans need identification to enter Canada, don't they?

5. Ice hockey is popular in Canada, isn't it?

6. Toronto isn't the capital of Canada, is it?

7. People in Quebec can't speak English, can they?

8. Niagara Falls isn't in Canada, is it?

9. There was a great fire in Vancouver in 1886, wasn't there?

10. Canada doesn't border Alaska, does it?

Now check the intonation on page 74. Sit with another student and practice saying the tag questions with the correct intonation. The answers to the questions are on page 75.

H. FILL IN THE TAG *Fill in the correct tag. Then read each question to a partner, using rising or falling intonation according to the answers you expect.*

1. You are studying English, _____ ?

2. You will be in class tomorrow, _____ ?

3. Our teacher is from the United States, _____ ?

4. This classroom isn't large, _____ ?

5. You're hungry, _____ ?

6. We're not from North America, _____ ?

7. We don't have English class every day, _____ ?

8. It wasn't snowing yesterday morning, _____ ?

9. We didn't come to class late today, _____ ?

10. I can't leave class early today, _____ ?

Working Together

A. YES/NO QUESTIONS *Read the questions and write two more in each category.*

Are you going to __visit a friend_____ this weekend?

Are you going to __take a vacation_____ this summer?

Are you going to _____ tomorrow?

Are you going to _____ in a few months?

Were you __on time_____ this morning?

Were you __at a party_____ last night?

Were you _____ last weekend?

Were you _____ ?

Do you __speak English_____ ?

Do you __study in the library_____ ?

Do you _____ ?

Do you _____ ?

Did you __live in another city_____ ?

Did you __write a letter last weekend__ ?

Did you _____ ?

Did you _____ ?

Are you __wear_____ing contact lenses?

Are you _____ ing French?

Are you _____ ?

Are you _____ ?

Will you __get married_____ next year?

Will you __buy something_____ new next week?

Will you _____ in three years?

Will you _____ by 2005?

In a group of three to four students, take turns asking each other your questions. Use the answers below.

Yes, I do.	Yes, I will.	Yes, I did.	Yes, I am.	Yes, I was.
No, I don't.	No, I won't	No, I didn't.	No, I'm not.	No, I wasn't.

■ B. FAMOUS CANADIANS *Working with a partner or a group of students, can you match each Canadian with his/her profession?*

Famous Canadian	Profession
Dan Aykroyd	actor
Kurt Browning	director
James Cameron	hockey player
Celine Dion	ice skater
Michael J. Fox	musician
Wayne Gretzky	singer
Alanis Morrissette	
Oscar Peterson	

Can you answer these questions about the famous Canadians?

1. Who starred in the *Back to the Future* movies?
2. Who recorded "Because You Loved Me"?
3. Who won an Olympic medal?
4. Who starred in *Ghost Busters*?
5. Who directed *Terminator*?
6. Who won a Stanley Cup championship?
7. Who plays jazz?
8. Who won a Grammy* Award in 1996?

*A music industry award.

The answers to the questions are on page 75.

■ C. TAG QUESTIONS *Fill in the blanks with the names of different classmates. Then, with a partner, ask and answer the questions. Practice the rising or falling intonation.*

1. _____ is from China, isn't she?

2. _____ has a job, doesn't he?

3. _____ and _____ speak Spanish, don't they?

4. _____ is sitting near the door, isn't he?

5. _____ doesn't play soccer, does he?

6. _____ didn't live in Montreal, did she?

7. _____ won't have a test tomorrow, will we?

8. _____ can't play the piano, can he?

Write two more tag questions about your classmates.

D. STUDENT TO STUDENT

Student A: *Read questions 1–4 below to* **Student B.** *Listen carefully and write the correct answer.*
Student B: *Turn to page 191.*

1. Which oceans border Canada?

   _____

2. Canada is the largest country in the world, isn't it?

   _____

3. How long is the United States - Canadian border?

   _____

4. What are Canada's official languages?

   _____

Now listen to **Student B** *read questions 5–8.* *Give the correct answer from the choices below.* *Then write the questions.* *Be careful!* *The questions are not in order.*

   _____

No, they don't. They settle in Ontario, Quebec, and British Columbia.

   _____

No, it isn't. It's Ottawa.

   _____

More than 60%.

   _____

Toronto, Montreal, and Vancouver.

■ A. VANCOUVER'S FESTIVALS AND SPECIAL EVENTS *Read the information in the chart about some of the festivals and special events in Vancouver.*

Month	Name of Event	Activities
January	Polar Bay Swim	More than 3,000 people swim in English Bay.
February	Chinese New Year	A parade in Chinatown; colorful dragons
May	Vancouver's Children's Festival	Crafts, theater, music, puppets, and dance
June	International du Maurier Jazz Festival	Artists from all over the world play jazz and blues.
July	Canada Day	Picnics, parades, and fireworks
August	Powell Street Festival	Costumes, Sumo wrestling, food, and music from all over Asia
December	First Night	Indoor and outdoor entertainment

*Fill in the missing question words and verbs. Answer the questions with the information from the chart. There are **yes/no** questions and **wh-** questions.*

1. _____ _____ people celebrate the holiday with a cold swim? In _____ .

2. _____ many Vancouverites celebrate Chinese New Year? _____, they _____ .

3. _____ _____ the Yang family see fireworks? In _____ .

4. _____ the Jazz Festival in April? _____, it _____ . It's in _____ .

5. _____ _____ children enjoy crafts, theater, and dance? In _____ .

6. _____ Vancouverites celebrating Canada Day this month? _____, they _____ .

7. _____ are Vancouverites _____ _____ celebrate next month? _____ .

8. _____ holiday _____ Vancouverites celebrate in _____ ? _____ .

9. _____ the Yang family _____ _____ see dragon parades next month? _____ , they _____ .

10. _____ the Powell Street Festival in August? _____ , _____ _____ .

■ B. WRITE THE QUESTION *Write questions with these cues. Then write the answers.*

1. who / your teacher?

   _____

   _____

2. who / immigrate / to this country with you?

   _____

   _____

3. where / you / live?

   _____

   _____

4. when / you / come / to this country?

   _____

   _____

5. what / your native language?

   _____

   _____

6. how / you / feel / today?

   _____

   _____

7. what / you / do / right now?

   _____

   _____

8. what kind of music / you / like?

   _____

   _____

9. whom / you / usually / go / to the movies with?

   _____

   _____

10. how many people / in your family?

   _____

   _____

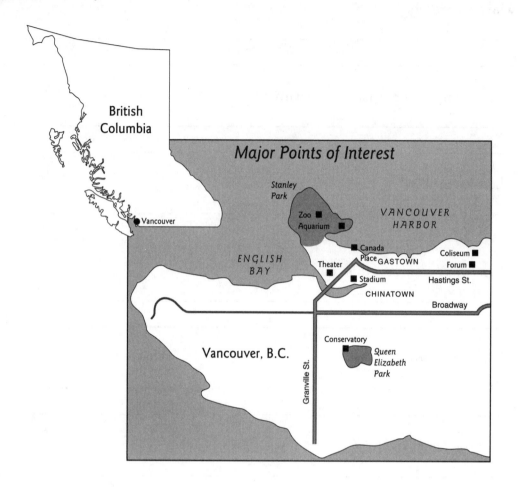

The Yangs are now in Vancouver staying with Victor, William's younger brother. Victor and his family moved to Vancouver three years ago.

Victor decided to move to Vancouver after he visited the city on a business trip. He liked the cleanliness, the natural setting, and the economic opportunities. At first, his wife, Lin, didn't want to come, but after a few months she met a few other immigrants from Hong Kong. They introduced her to more people in the neighborhood. Now Lin likes Vancouver very much, and she has found a job. She works three mornings a week at her daughter's elementary school. There are many other children there who speak Cantonese or Mandarin, so the school needs experienced teachers like Lin, who can speak both languages.

Right now, Victor and Lin are taking William and his family to see some of the sights in Vancouver. They visited Granville Island this morning. They walked around in the Public Market and enjoyed looking at the local and imported fruits, vegetables, and other foods and flowers. They decided to have some tea at an outdoor cafe and watch the boats come into the harbor.

It's 12:00, and now they're on their way to Gastown, the oldest part of Vancouver. There, they're going to take a trolley tour around the city. They're going to stop by Queen Elizabeth Park, the Rose Garden, which has three hundred species of roses, and the zoo.

They're also going to stop for a few hours in Chinatown to have a late lunch with some of their friends. William and his family are having a wonderful time, and they can't wait until Victor and his family come to San Francisco so that they can show them around their city.

1. _____?

   Because of the cleanliness, setting, and economic opportunities.

2. _____?

   No, she didn't.

3. Whom _____?

   Other immigrants from Hong Kong.

4. How _____?

   Three mornings a week.

5. What kind _____?

   Experienced teachers.

6. What _____?

   Going to see some of the sights.

7. What _____?

   Visited Granville Island and the Public Market.

8. Where _____?

   To Gastown.

9. How many _____?

   Three hundred.

10. How long _____?

    A few hours.

11. With whom _____?

    With some of their friends.

12. _____?

    Yes, they are.

Having Fun with the Language

A. TWENTY QUESTIONS *Divide into groups of four or five students. One student will pretend to be a famous person (an actor, politician, athlete, singer, etc.). The others in the group ask* **yes/no** *questions and try to guess who the famous person is.*

B. YOUR FAMILY *Bring in a photograph of you and your family at a special event (a wedding, a birthday party, etc.). In a group of four to five students, ask one another questions about the pictures. Use the past and present tenses.*

C. PICK A PROVINCE *Go to the library and select an encyclopedia, almanac, or other reference guide. Look up Canada. Select a province or territory that you would like to report on to your classmates. Look for details. Pick out four topics from the categories below, and find three facts about each category. Then write a short report about that province.*

Categories

climate	sports and recreation
population	land (geography)
size	tourist attractions
history	culture (theater, art, museums, etc.)
industries	cities

Grammar Summary

I. *Yes/no questions*

You are a student.	→	Are you a student?
She is jogging.	→	Is she jogging?
They were tired.	→	Were they tired?
They are going to watch TV.	→	Are they going to watch TV?
We study every day.	→	Do we study every day?
I had a test yesterday.	→	Did you have a test yesterday?
She will get married soon.	→	Will she get married soon?

■ 2. *Who* (as subject): *who* + singular verb

When *who* replaces a subject, it takes a singular verb.

Who is a student?

Who is jogging?

Who is going to watch TV?

Who will win the lottery?

Who studies every day?

Who had a test yesterday?

■ 3. *Whom/who* (as object)

Whom and *who* can both refer to the object. Both are used in speaking and in writing, but *whom* is considered more formal. *Whom* is often used with a preposition.

Bill is going to study with his friend. → **Whom** is he going to study with?

With whom is he going to study?

Who is he going to study with?

Bill studies with his friend. → **Whom** does he study with?

With whom does he study?

Who does he study with?

■ 4. *Whose* questions

Whose refers to possession. A singular or a plural noun can follow *whose.*

Whose books are those?

Whose advice will you follow?

■ 5. *Wh* questions

Where were you yesterday?

What is he doing?

When are they going to leave?

How did she get here?

Where do you work?

Why won't you come to the party?

▩ 6. Tag questions

Tag questions have two types of intonation, rising or falling. Falling intonation shows that the speaker expects an affirmative answer. Rising intonation shows that the speaker is not sure about the answer.

Your name is Marie, **isn't it?**

Your favorite sport wasn't baseball, **was it?**

We're having a good time, **aren't we?**

They have a pet, **don't they?**

She didn't drive, **did she?**

It isn't going to rain, **is it?**

He won't go to school tomorrow, **will he?**

Answers for Grammar In Action C. Yes/No Questions, page 61

1. Yes, it is.
2. No, it isn't. The population is **over 450,000.**
3. No, it isn't. Twenty-five percent of the population is **Asian.**
4. Yes, it does.
5. Yes, it does.
6. No, it isn't. It is one of Canada's **largest** industrial centers.
7. Yes, there are.
8. Yes, it was.
9. No, it isn't. Vancouver's Chinatown is the **second largest** in North America.

Answers for Grammar in Action G. Listen: Tag Questions, page 64 (Intonation)

1. The Yangs live in San Francisco, don't they? ↘
2. Canada has two official languages, doesn't it? ↗
3. Canada was first settled by the French, wasn't it? ↗
4. Americans need identification to enter Canada, don't they? ↘
5. Ice hockey is popular in Canada, isn't it? ↘
6. Toronto isn't the capital of Canada, is it? ↗
7. People in Quebec can't speak English, can they? ↗
8. Niagara Falls isn't in Canada, is it? ↗
9. There was a great fire in Vancouver in 1886, wasn't there? ↘
10. Canada doesn't border Alaska, does it? ↗

Answers for Grammar in Action G. Listen: Tag Questions, page 64 (Information)

1. Yes.
2. Yes.
3. Yes.
4. Yes.
5. Yes.
6. No.
7. Yes.
8. Yes. It's in both Canada and the U.S.
9. Yes.
10. Yes.

Answers for Working Together, B. Famous Canadians, page 66

Dan Aykroyd—actor
Kurt Browning—ice skater
James Cameron—director
Celine Dion—singer
Michael J. Fox—actor
Wayne Gretzky—hockey player
Alanis Morrissette—singer
Oscar Peterson—musician (jazz)

1. Michael J. Fox
2. Celine Dion
3. Kurt Browning
4. Dan Aykroyd
5. James Cameron
6. Wayne Gretzky
7. Oscar Peterson
8. Alanis Morrissette

6 **Plans and Possibilities**

Modals of possibility: *May, Might, Could, Must*

 A. LISTEN: RETIREMENT PLANS: *WILL AND MAY* *Jack is going to retire next month. Listen to this conversation between Jack and a co-worker. Complete each sentence with **will/won't** or **may/might**.*

1. Jack _will_____ travel.

2. Jack _____ take a cruise to Alaska.

3. Jack _____ visit Italy.

4. He _____ visit a friend in Peru.

To show certainty...
He will...
He won't...
To show possibility...
He may...
He might...

5. He _____ paint his house.

6. He _____ sell his house.

7. He _____ move to Florida when he is older.

8. He _____ move to Florida now.

9. He _____ look for an apartment or a condo.

10. He _____ buy a new fishing rod.

12. He _____ buy a small boat.

■ B. QUESTIONS ABOUT THE FUTURE *Use the cues below to ask other students questions about their future plans. Answer with an expression from the box.*

join a health club?

Q: Will you join a health club?   A: I might.

1. move this year?
2. fly someplace this year?
3. graduate from college?
4. get a pet?
5. give a party soon?

6. win the lottery?
7. live to be one hundred?
8. buy a computer?
9. travel around the world?
10. start to exercise?

To show certainty...
Yes, I will...
No, I won't...
To show possibility...
I might.
I may.

■ C. *MAY AND MIGHT* *Complete these sentences with a future possibility using **might** or **may**.*

May/Might: **Future Possibility**
May and *might* show possibility in the future.
He **may travel** to Hawaii.
I **might take** a class this summer.

1. If I don't study for the next test, __I might fail it.__

2. If I save $5,000, _____ .

3. When I have some free time, _____ .

4. After I finish this course, _____ .

5. If I don't feel well tomorrow, _____ .

6. If it's a beautiful day tomorrow, _____ .

7. When I retire, _____ .

■ D. *MAY AND MIGHT:* CONTINUOUS *Answer these questions about yourself in the continuous with* **might** *or* **may.**

Q: What will Jack be doing at this time next year?

A: He **may be working** part time, or he **might be traveling.**

1. Where will you be living next year?
2. What will you be studying in the future?
3. Where will you be working in two years?
4. What kind of car will you be driving next year?
5. What will you be doing this summer?
6. What will you be doing tonight at midnight?
7. What will you be doing this Sunday morning?

> *May/Might:* **Continuous**
> The continuous form can show present or future possibility.
>   He **may be watching** TV.
>   I **might be leaving** on Friday.

■ E. POSSIBILITY: PRESENT *Give two possible explanations for each situation. Use* **may, might,** *or* **could.**

> **Present Possibility**
> *May, might,* and *could* all express possibility in the present.
>   He **may have** a headache.
>   He **may not understand**.
>   He **might need** an appointment.
>   He **could be** worried.

1. The teacher is late today. Where is she?

   a. She could be stuck in traffic. _____

   b. _____

2. George is trying to get to sleep, but he can't.

   a. _____

   b. _____

3. Gina is baby-sitting for her one-year-old nephew. He's crying, but Gina doesn't know what the problem is.

   a. _____

   b. _____

4. Susan is trying a new recipe for dinner, but her children and her husband don't like it.

   a. _____

   b. _____

F. MUST: LOGICAL CONCLUSION Read each situation and complete the sentences with may/might or must. *Some of the sentences are negative.*

> **Must: Logical Conclusion**
> **Must** expresses a logical conclusion based on facts.
> He's holding his head and taking an aspirin.
> He **must have** a headache.

1. Jack walks three miles a day. He ___might___ be concerned about his health.

2. He also swims a mile each morning and lifts weights. He ___must___ be in good shape.

3. Jack has a fishing rod. He _____ fish a lot.

4. His fishing rod is old and broken. He _____ fish very often.

5. Jack has several books about birds and a pair of powerful binoculars. He _____ be a serious bird watcher.

6. Jack only has one pot and one plate in his kitchen. He _____ cook a lot. He _____ eat out a lot.

7. Jack is looking at brochures of China in a travel agency. He _____ go to China next year.

8. Jack is getting a new passport picture. He _____ need to renew his passport.

Working Together

A. FUTURE POSSIBILITIES Sit in a small group and answer these questions about your group members. *Then give two or three possibilities for their futures.*

> **EXAMPLE**
>
> Who has a boyfriend? Bianca does.
> She **might continue** to date him for a long time.
> She **may meet** someone new in one of her classes.

1. Who has a girlfriend/boyfriend?
2. Who is trying to decide on a major or career?
3. Who has a vacation coming up?
4. Who isn't too happy with his/her present job?
5. Who is going to start exercising?

> Write two more facts about people in your group. Give future possibilities.

B. SITUATIONS

*First, discuss what is happening in each of these pictures right now. Then decide what **might** happen.*

1.

2.

C. THE OPTIMIST AND THE PESSIMIST

An optimist looks at the positive side of life and expects the best. A pessimist looks at the negative side and expects the worst. Read the optimist's prediction. Then give the pessimist's point of view.

Optimist

A: It's going to be beautiful tomorrow.

A: I'm going to pass my math test.

A: We'll be able to get good seats for the concert.

Pessimist

B: You never know. It might rain.

B: Be careful. You might fail it.

B: You're dreaming. We might not be able to get any seats at all.

1. I'm going to lose ten pounds.
2. We're going to have a great time at the party.
3. I'm going to meet a wonderful man/woman this year.
4. I'm going to get a promotion at work.
5. Don't worry. We're going to catch the bus.
6. There isn't going to be much traffic. We'll be home in an hour.
7. I'm going to graduate in two years.
8. Keep looking. You'll find your keys.
9. The plane will arrive on time.
10. Our team is going to win the game.

Give an optimist's view and a pessimist's view about the weather.

D. STUDENT TO STUDENT *You each have information about five different people or places. Read your sentences about each person or situation. Put the information together and make a logical conclusion about each person or situation. Write your conclusion with **must**.*

Student A: Read the sentences on page 190.
Student B: Read the sentences on page 192.

1. Elena _____.

2. Armin _____.

3. Alex _____.

4. That restaurant _____.

5. New Jersey _____.

6. Kyoko _____.

Practicing on Your Own

A. THE WORLD IN 2050 *How will the world be different in the future? Write these possibilities with **may** or **might**.*

1. Perhaps scientists will find a cure for AIDS.

   Scientists might find a cure for AIDS. _____

2. Perhaps astronauts will reach Mars.

   _____

3. Maybe all homes will have computers.

   _____

4. Maybe there will be a vaccine against the common cold.

   _____

5. Perhaps more cars will be battery operated.

   _____

6. Maybe the average life expectancy will reach eighty.

_____

7. Perhaps there will be a thirty-hour work week.

_____

8. Perhaps there will be a woman president of the United States.

_____

9. Maybe all politicians will be honest.

_____

> Write two more sentences describing how
> the world might be different in the future.

■ B. WHAT'S THE REASON? *Read each problem or situation. Write a possible reason for each using* **may, may not, might, might not,** *or* **could.**

1. I get headaches when I read.

   You might need glasses. _____

2. Our teacher is late.

   _____

3. Armando's wife bought him a CD for his birthday. He's returning it to the store.

   _____

4. It's midnight. Tommy, three years old, is sitting up in bed and crying.

   _____

5. Joy is very intelligent, but she doesn't do well in school.

   _____

6. Henry bought a Cadillac last year, but he's thinking of trading it in and buying a Honda.

   _____

7. George and Bob are eating dinner at an expensive restaurant. They look annoyed.

   _____

8. A student just asked the teacher if he could leave class early today.

_____

Sharing Our Stories

Read Maria's story as she writes about her pregnancy and future plans.

My name is Maria and I'm from Colombia. I'm expecting my third child. According to the doctor, the baby's going to be born in July. My husband is very excited, just like me. We have two other children, a boy who is ten years old and a girl who is five. My daughter thinks that I will have a girl. My son thinks we might have to move to a bigger apartment. We might not have enough room for another child. I think we may have enough room.

My mother-in-law is going to come in July to help me with the new baby. She may stay three months or longer. After the baby arrives, I'm going to stop working for a while. I'm not sure how long I will stay home. I might stay home for three months, or I might stay home longer. Right now, I'm not worrying about work; I'm thinking about the new baby and knitting baby hats, booties, and blankets.

Maria Zamudio, Colombia

Write about your future plans. Are you going to graduate, go to college, move, look for a new job, take a vacation? Write about some plans that you have; you don't need to be certain of all the details.

Having Fun with the Language

■ **A. NEWS STORY** *Bring in a current news story about a political election, crime, local issue, etc. What might happen in the next few days or weeks?*

■ **B. NAME THE OCCUPATION** *Sit in small groups of three or four students. Think of five occupations. List four items that a person in that occupation wears or uses. Join with another group and read your lists. Can the other group guess the occupation?*

> **EXAMPLE**
>
> 1: hammer, saw, nails, lumber   He **must** be a carpenter.
>
> 2: microscope, blood, white uniform, slides   She **might** be a laboratory technician.
>
> 3: needle, thread, cloth, buttons   He **must** be a tailor.

Grammar Summary

■ **1.** *May and might*

Use *may* or *might* to express possibility in the present and the future.

Jack **might buy** a computer.

Jack **might not work** part time.

The continuous form shows present continuous or future possibility.

Jack **might be cleaning** out his office.

Note the difference between *may be* and *maybe*

Maybe expresses possibility. Use *maybe* at the beginning of a sentence.

Jack **may** *be* excited.	(Verb = modal + *be*)
Maybe Jack *is* excited.	(Verb = *is*)
Incorrect: He maybe sick.	(There is no verb in this sentence!)

▪ 2. Could

Could expresses a possibility in the present tense.

George wants to find a new roommate. His present roommate **could be** messy.

Note: **Couldn't** shows impossibility.

She **couldn't be** his sister. He's an only child.

▪ 3. Must

Must (affirmative) expresses a logical conclusion based on facts.

Maria had a bad cold yesterday. She's absent today. She **must be** home sick.

Pedro is returning a present, a CD by Julio Iglesias. He **must not like** Julio Iglesias.

7 Driving

Modals of Necessity and Advice: *Must, Have to, (Not) Have to, Can, Should, Had Better*

Grammar in Action

A. LISTEN: A DRIVER'S LICENSE *Listen to Teresa, who hopes to get her driver's license soon. Look at the chart and fill in the missing information about obtaining a license in her state.*

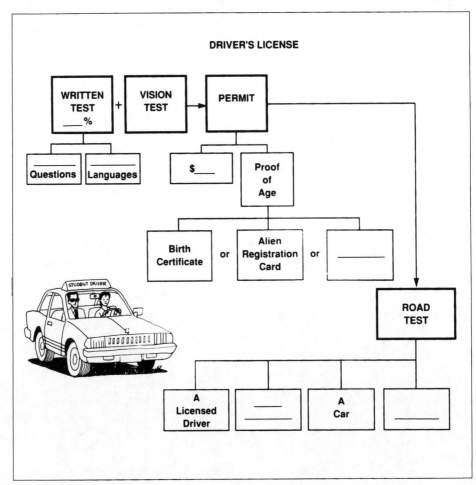

■ B. GETTING THE FACTS
Read each sentence about the process of getting a license. Circle **T** *for true or* **F** *for false. If the answer is false, give the correct information.*

T   F   1. Teresa must take two tests to get her permit.

T   F   2. Teresa has to take the test in English.

T   F   3. Teresa must get 90% on the written test.

T   F   4. Teresa must get a permit before she takes the road test.

T   F   5. Teresa must pay for her permit.

T   F   6. Teresa has to show proof of age.

T   F   7. Teresa must show her birth certificate for proof of age.

T   F   8. Teresa must buy a new car to get a license.

T   F   9. Teresa has to have a full-time job to get a license.

T   F   10. Teresa must go to the road test with a licensed driver.

> Talk about getting a license in your state. How is the process the same or different?

■ C. *MUST/HAVE TO/MUST NOT*
Using **must**, **have to**, *or* **must not**, *state the traffic law regarding each of the sentences below.*

EXAMPLE

Stop at a stop sign.   You **must stop** at a stop sign.

                       You **have to stop** at a stop sign.

Go through a red light.   You **must not go** through a red light.

1. Pass cars on the right.
2. Pay traffic fines.
3. Drink and drive.
4. Register your car.
5. Drive over the speed limit.
6. Leave the scene of an accident.
7. Wear your seat belt.
8. Drive over 25 mph in a school zone.
9. Stop for a school bus with flashing lights.
10. Drive without a license.

Have to / Must		
Have to and *must* express obligation or necessity.		
I Drivers	have to	stop at a red light.
She A driver	has to	drive at the speed limit.

Must not		
Must not expresses that an action is unlawful or not permitted.		
I He Drivers	must not	drive without a license.

87

D. DOESN'T HAVE TO
Use **don't have to** or **doesn't have to** and restate each of these regulations for learners and drivers.

Don't have to / Doesn't have to		
Don't have to shows that an action is not necessary.		
I Drivers	don't have to	take a hearing test.
He A driver	doesn't have to	take the test in English.

EXAMPLE

It's not necessary for a learner to own a car.

A learner **doesn't have to own** a car.

1. It's not necessary for a learner to take the test in English.
2. It's not necessary for learners to be American citizens.
3. It's not necessary for a learner to get 100 percent on the written test.
4. It's not necessary for a learner to be twenty-one to get a license.
5. It's not necessary for a driver to have perfect vision.
6. It's not necessary for a learner to pay $20.00 for a license.
7. It's not necessary for a learner to show a birth certificate.
8. It's not necessary for learners to go to private driving school.
9. It's not necessary for a learner to make an appointment to take the written test.
10. It's not necessary for drivers to be able to speak English.

E. LISTEN: CAN AND CAN'T
Listen to Marcus talk about his driving experience. Complete these sentences with **can** *or* **can't.**

Pronunciation	
I can **drive.**	Stress the main verb.
I **can't** drive.	Stress **can't.**

Can / Cannot	
Can shows ability or possibility. **Can** also shows that an action is lawful or permitted.	
I	can drive a truck.
She	can't drive without a license.

1. I _____ drive very well.

2. I _____ drive only with a licensed driver in the car.

3. I _____ back up.

4. I _____ parallel park.

5. I _____ drive on a busy highway.

Now, complete these sentences about yourself. Then read your sentences to a partner. Your partner will fill in **can** *or* **can't.**

1. I _____ change a flat tire.   My partner _____ change a flat tire.

2. I _____ parallel park.   My partner _____ parallel park.

3. I _____ drive a stick shift.   My partner _____ drive a stick shift.

4. I _____ read a map in English.   My partner _____ read a map in English.

5. I _____ afford a new car.   My partner _____ afford a new car.

■ F. SHOULD *Check if you agree or disagree with each statement. Then discuss your reasons in a small group.*

Should
Should expresses opinion or advice.

I		
He	should	go to driving school.
Drivers		

	Agree	Disagree
1. Drivers should drive more carefully near elementary schools.	❏	❏
2. Teenagers shouldn't get their licenses until they are eighteen.	❏	❏
3. Drivers with small children should put their children in the back seat.	❏	❏
4. People over eighty shouldn't drive anymore.	❏	❏
5. Drivers should not eat and drive at the same time.	❏	❏
6. All cars should have telephones.	❏	❏
7. All passengers in a car should wear seat belts.	❏	❏
8. All drivers should have car insurance.	❏	❏

■ G. HAD BETTER *Each sentence below gives a warning. Complete each sentence with **had better** or give a future result.*

Had better
Had better gives strong advice or a warning.

You	had better	slow down.

1. You __had better slow down_____ , or you'll get a speeding ticket.

2. You _____ , or you'll get a parking ticket.

3. You'd better put your packages in the trunk, or _____ .

4. You _____ , or someone will steal your car.

5. You'd better roll up the back window, or _____ .

6. You'd better pay that parking ticket, or _____ .

7. You _____ , or we'll run out of gas.

What's the difference?
You should slow down.
You'd better slow down.

Working Together

A. TRAFFIC SIGNS
Sit in a small group and give the traffic rule for each sign. Use **must, have to** *or* **must not.**

You **must stay** to the right.

> Draw three common traffic signs and give the traffic rule for each.

B. IT'S THE LAW
Read each sentence; then say each sentence a second time, substituting **has to, have to, doesn't have to, don't have to, must,** *or* **must not** *for the words in italics. You will need to change the wording in some of the sentences.*

EXAMPLE

It is the law to register your car.   You **must register** your car.

1. *It is not necessary for* Teresa to renew her license in person.
2. *It is the law for* you to carry your license with you when you drive.
3. *It is against the law for* you to leave the scene of an accident.
4. *It is against the law for* Teresa to drink any alcoholic beverage while driving.
5. *It is necessary for* Teresa to have auto insurance.
6. *It is necessary for* you to put on your headlights when it's dark.
7. *It is the law for* you to wear a helmet when you ride a motorcycle.
8. *It is against the law for* you to let children under five ride without car seats.
9. *It is necessary for* Teresa to drive carefully in bad weather.
10. *It is not necessary for* you to have air bags on both sides of your car.
11. *It is not necessary for* Teresa to have a radio in her car.
12. *It is the law for* Teresa to always drive with a licensed driver until she gets her license.

Driver:	What's the problem, officer?
Officer:	Your headlight is broken.
Driver:	Yes, but it just happened last weekend. I'm going to take it to the service station tomorrow.
Officer:	Let me see your license and registration.
Driver:	Here's my license, but I left my registration in my wife's car.
Officer:	Get out of the car, please.
Driver:	Uh, oh.

■ D. DISCUSSION *Discuss these questions in a small group.*

1. Have you ever received a traffic ticket in this country? Explain what happened.
2. Did you ever receive a traffic ticket in your native country? Explain what happened.
3. In this state, what is the speed limit in the following areas?
   a. highway   b. local road   c. school zone
4. In this state, what is the law for . . . ?
   a. seat belts   b. car seats   c. children on bicycles
5. In this state, what is the penalty for . . . ?
   a. driving without a license   c. driving without wearing a seat belt
   b. driving over the speed limit   d. driving under the influence of alcohol

Practicing on Your Own

■ A. TRAFFIC REGULATIONS *Fill in the blank in each sentence with the correct modal.*

must   has to   doesn't have to
must not   have to   don't have to

1. You _don't have to_ take the written test in English.

2. You _____ drive over the speed limit.

3. You _____ get a permit before you can get your license.

4. You _____ stop at a red light.

5. All drivers _____ drive carefully.

6. Children under five _____ ride in car seats in the back seat.

7. Children between six and sixteen _____ wear seat belts.

8. You _____ have a cellular phone in your car.

9. You _____ drive over 25 miles per hour in a school zone.

10. Drivers _____ wash their cars once a month.

11. Teresa _____ take a breath test if a police officer catches her driving under the influence of alcohol.

12. Teresa _____ take a vision test.

13. You _____ stop when a school bus loads or unloads children.

14. Teresa _____ stop at a green light.

15. Children, twelve and under, _____ wear helmets when they ride their bicycles.

■ B. TEENAGE DRIVING LIMITS *Limits on teenage driving vary from state to state. Look at the chart and complete the information about your state in the last column.*

Limits on Teenage Driving by State

	CA	FL	MA	NY	OR	PA	MY STATE
Learner's permit required	☑	☑	☑	☑	☐	☑	☐
No driving at night	☐	☑	☑	☑	☐	☑	☐
Parental supervision of driving	☑	☐	☐	☐	☐	☐	☐
Driver's education required	☑	☐	☑	☑	☐	☑	☐
More training required after accident	☐	☐	☑	☑	☑	☐	☐
Seat belts	☑	☑	☑	☑	☑	☑	☐

Source: National Highway Traffic Safety Administration.

Complete the sentences according to the information in the chart Use **can, cannot, must, must not,** *or* **don't have to/doesn't have to.**

1. In California, teenage drivers ___have to_____ wear seat belts.

2. In Florida, a teenage driver _____ have parental supervision.

3. In Florida, teenage drivers _____ wear seat belts.

4. In Massachusetts, teenage drivers _____ obtain a learner's permit.

5. In Massachusetts and New York, a teenage driver _____ get a license without a driver's education course.

6. In New York, parents _____ accompany teenagers who drive.

7. In Oregon, teenage drivers _____ drive at night.

8. In Oregon, a teenage driver _____ take more training after an accident.

9. In Pennsylvania, teenage drivers _____ drive at night, but they _____ drive without parental supervision.

> What are the limits on teenage driving in your state?

■ C. MODAL REVIEW *Compare the driving rules in the state you live in now and your country. Add an appropriate verb when necessary.*

can/can't   must   must not   don't have to

1. In this state, I _____ a seat belt.

2. In my country, I _____ a seat belt.

3. In this state, children _____ in car seats.

4. In my country, children _____ in car seats.

5. In this state, drivers _____ without auto insurance.

6. In my country, drivers _____ without auto insurance.

7. In this state, you _____ obtain a license until you are _____ years old.

8. In my country, you _____ obtain a license until you are _____ years old.

> Make one more comparison between this state and your country.

Sharing Our Stories

My cousin, Tony, got in a lot of trouble last summer. Tony is eighteen and in college. He doesn't have his own car; he drives his parents' car.

Tony went to a party and drank three or four cans of beer. When he was driving home, a police car signaled him to pull over. Tony had to show the police officer his license and get out of the car. The police officer smelled the beer on his breath. Tony had to walk a straight line and take a Breathalyzer test. The police decided that he had above the legal limit of alcohol, so they arrested him and took him to the police station. After they arrived at the police station, Tony called his parents. His parents had to come to the station to pick him up so he didn't have to spend the night in jail.

The next month, Tony had to go to court. This was his first offense, so he didn't have to give up his license, but the judge put him on probation for six months. He had to pay a $500 fine. He also had to spend thirty hours at a local boys' club as a youth volunteer. My aunt and uncle were furious at him. Their insurance went up almost $700. They don't let him drive their car anymore, and he was grounded for two months.

Nelson Morales

Did you ever receive a ticket? Did anyone you know ever receive a ticket? Describe the situation in detail. What was the fine or other punishment?

A. THE LOCAL NEWS *Look in the local newspaper and find a report about one of the following topics. Read the article, and then summarize the article for your classmates in a class presentation.*

1. A traffic accident
2. Driving safety
3. New driving rules
4. Air bags
5. Children and cars

Grammar Summary

1. *Have to* and *must*

Use *have to* and *must* to express obligation or necessity. They often state rules, laws, or regulations.

I **must stop** at a red light.   I **have to wear** a seat belt.   He **has to pay** his traffic ticket.

2. *Don't have to*

Don't have to shows that an action is not necessary.

You **don't have to be** twenty-one to drive.   She **doesn't have to get** 100% on the written test.

3. *Must not* and *cannot*

Must not and *cannot* show that an action is unlawful or not permitted.

She **must not go through** a red light.   A driver **cannot leave** the scene of an accident.

4. *Can*

Can shows that an action is lawful or permitted. *Can* also expresses ability.

I **can take** the written test in Spanish.   I **can change** a flat tire.

5. *Should*

Should expresses advice or opinion.

I **should study** before I take the written test.   You **shouldn't take** the test in English.

6. *Had better*

Had better expresses strong advice or a warning.

You **had better slow** down, or you'll get a ticket.

8 Changes

Present Perfect

A. LISTEN: A PHONE CALL *Kathy and Selma haven't spoken for several months. Listen to their conversation.*

*Read each sentence. Circle **T** for **True** or **F** for **False**.*

T   F   1. Kathy and Selma haven't spoken for a long time.

T   F   2. The family has become very large.

T   F   3. The family has just had a reunion.

T   F   4. Angela has sent out the invitations already.

T   F   5. Selma has just become a grandmother.

T   F   6. Michael has just retired.

T   F   7. He has opened a small business.

> Underline the verbs in the present perfect tense. How do you form the present perfect?

B. FOR AND SINCE   *Circle **for** or **since** in the sentences below.*

For	Since
For shows an amount of time:	**Since** tells when an action started:
for a few days	since 1995
for three weeks	since Sunday
for two years	since she began her new job

1. Kathy and Selma haven't spoken   (for)   since   several months.

2. Michael has had a small business   **for**   since   January.

3. Barney and Gloria have been married   **for**   since   1950.

4. Jean has been a vegetarian   **for**   since   three years.

5. Henry has belonged to the volunteer fire department   **for**   since   1990.

6. Joanna has sold life insurance   **for**   since   ten years.

7. Rita has been divorced   **for**   since   six months.

8. Richard has owned his own business   **for**   since   he moved to Ohio.

9. Tom has been in college   **for**   since   six years.

10. Anna has walked two miles a day   **for**   since   she had her heart attack.

11. She has also followed a strict diet   **for**   since   three years.

12. Brian has played professional baseball   **for**   since   1995.

◼ C. PRESENT PERFECT TENSE *Write the past participle for each of the verbs below. A list of irregular past participles is in the appendix on page 187.*

buy _____bought_____   get _____

become _____   gain _____

change _____   grow _____

dye _____   have _____

enroll _____   lose _____

Present Perfect Tense		
I		
You		
We	have	
They		moved.
He		
She	has	
It		

Complete these sentences about the changes in the Clemens family with a verb from the list above. Use the present perfect form.

1. Simon _____has grown_____ a beard.

2. Theresa _____ a lot of weight.

3. Loretta and George _____ a divorce.

4. Uncle Bill _____ all his hair.

5. Julia and Mark _____ twins.

6. Mario _____ rich and famous.

7. Grandma _____ the most of all!

8. She _____ her hair and _____ a facelift.

9. Grandma _____ in art school.

10. She _____ a new red convertible.

◼ D. SINCE *"How has your life changed since . . . ?" Which of these sentences match the since clauses below?*

I haven't had a good night's sleep   I have lost 10 pounds   I've made several new friends

I have had several complaints from my neighbors   I haven't been able to concentrate on my studies

. . . . since I had the baby.   . . . . since I joined the health club.

. . . . since I fell in love.   . . . . since I bought a dog.

Now complete these sentences using the present perfect tense.

1. _____ since I came to the United States.

2. _____ since I got my driver's license.

3. _____ since he broke his arm.

4. _____ since she lost her job.

5. _____ since they got married.

■ **E. *ALREADY AND YET*** *Angela is planning a family reunion. On her "Things to Do" list, she has checked everything she has already done. Talk about each item on her list, using* **already** *or* **yet.**

Already
Already shows that an action is completed. It is used in affirmative sentences. Place **already** before the main verb or at the end of the sentence.
  She has **already** bought the invitations.
  She has bought the invitations **already**.

Yet
Yet shows the action has not yet started or is not completed. It is used in negative sentences. Place **yet** at the end of the sentence.
  She hasn't sent the invitations **yet.**

EXAMPLE

Angela has **already** formed a committee to help plan the reunion.

She hasn't sent the invitations **yet.**

	Things to Do
✓	form a committee to help plan the reunion
✓	set a date
	make the invitations on the computer
	find the addresses of relatives who have moved
	send the invitations
	plan the activities and games
	buy the decorations
✓	order the cake
	plan the menu
	buy a new grill
✓	hire two people to help cook, serve, and clean up

F. HOW LONG/HOW MANY *Ask questions with **How long** or **How many** to find out the following information about the students in your class.*

Who has lived in the United States the longest?

How long have you lived in the United States?

Who has traveled to the most countries?

How many countries have you traveled to?

1. Who has had a driver's license the longest?
2. Who has worked the longest?
3. Who has moved the most times?
4. Who has visited the most states?
5. Who has studied English the longest?
6. Who has eaten out the most times this week?
7. Who has been married the longest?
8. Who has been at his/her present job the longest?
9. Who has seen the most movies this month?
10. Who has had a computer the longest?

G. CONTRAST—PRESENT PERFECT AND PAST *Write the missing verb in the past or the present perfect. Explain the reason for your choice of each tense.*

Present Perfect vs. Past Tense
The **present perfect tense** tells about an action completed in the past, but the definite time is not stated or known.   They have moved.   The **past tense** tells about an action completed in the past. The time is stated or known.   They moved in February.

1. Dave moved into his new apartment four months ago.

   He ___has lived_____ (live) in his apartment for four months.

2. My mother and father _____ (get) married in 1950.

   They have been married since 1950.

3. I _____ (join) the Democratic party ten years ago.

   I have belonged to the Democratic party for ten years.

4. She began to work at the nursing home three years ago.

   She _____ (work) at the nursing home for three years.

5. Patty was a very good seamstress. She made all her own clothes.

   She _____ (made) any clothes since she started to work full time.

6. Sherry and Kathy met for the first time when they were in high school.

They _____ (be) best friends since that time.

7. Ricardo _____ (start) his diet two months ago.

He has lost ten pounds since he started his diet.

8. I _____ (take) my first art class five years ago.

I have taken art classes for five years.

9. He _____ (buy) a Ford Mustang in the 1970s.

He has taken very good care of the car. He _____ (drive) it for over twenty-five years!

10. Sofia had a heart attack two months ago.

She _____ (eat) any fried foods since then.

Working Together

A. FIND SOMEONE WHO... *Stand up, walk around the classroom, and ask your classmates these questions about changes in their lives in the last five years. Try to find someone who answers **Yes** to each item. Write that student's name on the line.*

> **EXAMPLE**
>
> Have you changed jobs?   No, I haven't.   (Continue to ask other students!)
> Have you changed jobs?   Yes, I have.   (Write that student's name.)

Have you . . .

1. change jobs?   _____

2. travel to another country?   _____

3. buy a house?   _____

4. join a club or an organization?   _____

5. get married?   _____

6. have a baby?   _____

7. be in an accident?   _____

*Now ask for some specific information and details from a student who answered **Yes** to one of the questions above.*

> **EXAMPLE**
>
> **A**: Have you changed jobs?   **B**: Yes, I have.
> **A**: Where do you work now?   **B**: I work as an operator for the telephone company.
> **A**: When did you start there?   **B**: I started two months ago.

B. GOALS *Before you came to the United States, what were three of your goals? Did you want to buy a house? Did you want to learn English? Write three of your goals below.*

My goals before I came to the United States:

1. _____

2. _____

3. _____

Read each goal to your group. tell if you have accomplished that goal since you came to the United States. Use **already** *or* **yet** *in your answer.*

■ **C. CHANGES** *Sit in a group of three students. Write five more sentences describing the changes in each set of pictures.*

Allan one year ago

Allan today

Allan has cut off his ponytail.

The back yard six months ago

The back yard today

They have built a deck.

D. STUDENT TO STUDENT

Student A: *Student B will read information about several people. Using the information, complete the sentences below with the verb in parentheses in the present perfect tense. Use a time expression, if needed.*
Student B: *Turn to page 192.*

Student A:

1. George and Barney _____have lived_____ (live) in Boston for _____ .

2. Maria _____ (live) in Chicago since _____ .

3. Ricardo _____ (be) in the United States since _____ .

4. We _____ (see) that movie yet.

5. My mother _____ (have) a cough for _____ .

Now change pages. **Student A** *will turn to page 192 and read the information (sentences 6 to 10).* **Student B** *will complete the sentences below.*

Student B:

6. I _____ (see) my brother for _____ .

7. Henry _____ (be) very sick.

8. Amy _____ (buy) her ticket already, but she

   _____ (find) her passport yet.

9. Sara _____ (work) at the post office since

   _____ .

10. I _____ (know) Thomas since _____ .

Practicing on Your Own

■ A. A CHANGED CITY
Last year, Tamara returned to her native city for the first time in ten years. Complete these sentences about the changes she saw. Use the present perfect tense.

1. Ten years ago, there were two doctors. Now there is a small clinic with six doctors. The health care system _has improved_____ (improve)

2. The population _____ from 25,000 to 47,000. (increase)

3. Many new restaurants _____. (open)

4. The unemployment rate _____ from 15 percent to 9 percent. (decrease)

5. Tourism _____ a big business. (become)

6. The city _____ fifty more police officers. (hire)

7. The crime rate _____ substantially. (drop)

8. Many new businesses _____ into the area because of the strong economy. (move)

9. Her quiet village _____ into a busy, noisy town. (change)

■ B. A CHANGED STUDENT
Tommy had a difficult first semester at college and is now on academic probation. But he's changed and become a serious student. Compare his first and second semesters, using the present perfect tense.

First Semester: The Old Tommy	Second Semester: The New Tommy
1. He missed ten days of school.	1. He has missed only one day.
2. He was late for all his classes.	2.
3. He failed every test.	3.
4. He didn't ask for extra help.	4.
5. He didn't do his homework.	5.
6. He failed two courses.	6.
7. He didn't study for the tests.	7.
8. He didn't write any papers.	8.

■ C. CONTRAST
Complete these conversations with the verb in the correct tense. You may use present continuous, present, past, future, or present perfect.

1. **A:** You look great!

   B: Thanks. I ___have been_____ (be) on a low-fat diet for six months. I _____ (lost) fifteen pounds so far.

2. **A:** My parents _____ just _____ . (retire)

   B: _____ they _____ (stay) in their house?

   A: No. It's for sale. They _____ (have) it on the market for six months, but they _____ (negative—sell) it yet.

3. **A:** How long _____ Richard and Ellen _____ (be) divorced?

   B: About one year.

   A: Why _____ she _____ (leave) him?

   B: I don't know. I _____ (negative—think) they were happy.

4. **A:** I _____ (live) in the city for ten years. And for ten years I _____ (complain) about the traffic and the noise. I _____ (negative—have) a good night's sleep in ages.

   B: Why don't you move?

   A: Well, I _____ (start) dating the man in the next apartment last year.

   B: Oh! That's why you _____ . (negative—move)

5. **A:** Hello, Amy! Look at you! You _____ (grow) up!

   B: The last time you _____ (see) me, I _____ (be) seventeen. Now I _____ (be) twenty-three.

   A: What _____ you _____ (do) now?

   B: I _____ (graduate) from college last year. I _____ (find) a job at an engineering company, and I _____ (be) there for about two months.

   A: One day, I _____ (hear) that you are the company president!

   B: Uncle George! No wonder you _____ always _____ (be) my favorite uncle!

Changes

I came to the United States from Poland four years ago. My life has changed a lot since I came here. In my country, I didn't work. I studied and I took care of my newborn son. My parents helped me a lot. When I came to America, everything changed.

At first, I had a problem with English. I couldn't understand people around me, so I had to go to school to learn how to communicate. The second problem I had was the loneliness. In Poland I had parents and friends whom I could count on and tell about my problems. In America, my husband and I were alone. We had to become adults right away. We had to find a place to live, and my husband had to find a job to get money for our bills and food. Our parents and all our friends were far away from us and couldn't help us anymore.

Now, many things have changed. I have been at college for about three years, and I have learned to communicate well in English. I have even gotten a part-time job working in an office at the college. My husband has found a good job that he likes. My son has learned English, but he hasn't forgotten Polish, and he has started kindergarten. This new life hasn't been easy, but right now, we feel better. We've made new friends and we feel comfortable.

Anna Blaszczyk, Poland

Having Fun with the Language

■ A. I'VE CHANGED! *Sit in a small group. Show one or two photos of yourself five or ten years ago. Tell your group how you have changed.*

■ B. MY HOMETOWN *If possible, sit with a group of students from your own country. Have any students returned for a visit? How has your country changed in the past few years?*

C. SENIOR CITIZENS *Interview a senior citizen, or ask your teacher to invite a senior citizen into class. Ask questions about that person's life fifty years ago, including information about education, recreation, transportation, and money. Then write a short paragraph describing how life has changed in the United States over the last fifty years.*

Grammar Summary

1. Present perfect

a. The present perfect tense talks about an action that started in the past and continues into the present. The action is not completed.

> He **has worked** at General Plastics for six years.
> They **have lived** in Linden since they came to the United States.

b. The present perfect also talks about past activities, but the time or date is not specified. If a specific past time is indicated, use the past tense.

> He **has opened** his own business.   (The time is not specified.)
> He **opened** his own business two months ago.   (A time is specified.)
> He **opened** his own business in 1996.   (A time is specified.)

c. *For* and *Since*

For shows an amount of time.

> **for** three weeks
> **for** two years

Since tells when an action started.

> **since** 1995
> **since** he came to the United States

d. *Already* and *Yet*

Already shows that the action has been completed.

> She has **already** planned the party.

Yet shows that the action has not been completed.

> She hasn't sent the invitations **yet.**

2. Statements

> I **have been** at my present job since 1995.
> They **have worked** at the library for two years.
> She **has lived** in the same apartment since she came to the United States.

3. *Yes/no* questions

> **Have** you **worked** at the company for a long time?   No, I **haven't.**
> **Has** he **gotten** married?   Yes, he **has**.

4. *How long/how many* questions

> **How long** have you lived in the United States?   For three years.
> **How many** times have you visited Disney World?   Just once.

9 Job Performance

Present Perfect with *Ever*; Adverbs of Frequency

A. A BUSY OFFICE
The office at CarCo Insurance is busy this morning. Use the verbs below to describe what each person is doing.

receive (a fax)	repair	take (a break)	drink	make (a copy)
speak	fill out (a form)	type (a letter)	address (an envelope)	

B. HOW MANY
Look at the office picture. What has each person accomplished so far this morning? Use the verbs from Exercise A to complete these sentences in the present perfect tense.

1. Harold _____*has made*_____ copies of twenty forms.

2. Jeff _____ six faxes. He _____ also
   _____ with three clients in person.

3. Three clients had accidents this past weekend. Ellen _____ three car
   insurance claim forms.

4. Mark _____ four breaks. He _____ six cups of coffee.

5. Melissa _____ two computers so far.

6. Katie _____ twenty envelopes to potential clients.

7. George _____ three cancellation letters to clients who have not paid
   their insurance premiums.

C. LISTEN: A NOTE FROM THE BOSS
Jeff works for CarCo Insurance. When he arrived at work this morning, there was a note on his e-mail asking him to see the boss at 2:00 this afternoon. Listen to his conversation with Katie, a co-worker. Then complete these sentences about Jeff's job performance with the correct adverb.

always	often	never	just	so far

1. Jeff has _____ left work early before.

2. He has _____ arrived on time.

3. He has _____ stayed late.

4. He has written fifteen new policies _____ this month.

5. He has _____ received an evaluation.

> **Vocabulary**
> sales figures
> new car policies
> complaints
> evaluation
> promote

■ D. JOB PERFORMANCE
Jeff has been an employee at CarCo Insurance for three years. Talk about his job performance. Use the present perfect tense, and place the adverb of frequency in the correct position in the sentence.

> **Adverbs of Frequency/Time Expressions**
>
> Place adverbs of frequency (e.g., **always, sometimes, often, never**) before the main verb:
>
> He has **always arrived** on time.
>
> He has **never had** a problem with a co-worker.
>
> Time expressions (e.g., **from time to time, so far this month**) are usually at the end of a sentence. Sometimes we use time expressions at the beginning.
>
> He has written fifteen new policies **so far this month.**
>
> He has attended training classes **from time to time.**
>
> **From time to time** he has attended training classes.

1. He has arrived late. (never)
2. He has missed work without notice. (never)
3. He has stayed late. (five times this month)
4. He has been polite and helpful to customers. (always)
5. He has trained new employees. (a few times)
6. He has managed the office. (never)
7. He has supervised new employees. (from time to time)
8. He has been a team player. (always)
9. He has made a mistake on a new policy. (rarely)
10. He has attended three sales meetings. (so far this year)

■ E. EMPLOYEE PERFORMANCE
These four insurance agents have been working for CarCo for one year or more. Look at the chart and answer questions about their job performance.

	Years at CarCo	Policies Last Year	Policies This Year to Date	Customer Complaints This Year
Jeff	3	125	43	2
Katie	1	67	40	5
George	4	55	12	0
Ellen	2	88	35	10

1. Who has worked at CarCo the longest?
2. How long has George worked there?
3. Is George the best agent at CarCo? Why or why not?

4. Who wrote the most policies last year? Who wrote the fewest?

5. Who has written the most policies so far this year?

6. Which agent has received the fewest complaints?

7. Ellen has sold many policies so far this year. Why is the boss dissatisfied with her performance?

8. Katie has worked at CarCo for only one year. How would you evaluate her performance?

■ F. MY TEACHER *Ask your teacher these questions about his or her work and interests.*

1. Have you ever worked in a different school?

2. Have you ever taught another subject?

3. Have you ever taught in another country?

4. Have you ever studied another language?

5. Have you ever had another kind of job?

6. Have you ever eaten _____ food?

7. Have you ever gone to a soccer game?

8. Have you ever visited Alaska?

9. Have you ever flown across the country?

10. Have you ever acted in a play?

> Ask your teacher two more questions about work or interests with "Have you ever...?"

Working Together

■ A. MY JOB *Sit in a group of three students. Use these phrases to talk about your job or the job performance of someone you know. Use an adverb or time expression: **always, never, sometimes, often, rarely, from time to time,** or **a few times.***

1. call in sick
2. take a personal day
3. work overtime
4. leave work early
5. work on a holiday

6. follow the safety regulations
7. receive a bonus
8. work a double shift
9. have a problem with a customer
10. complain to the boss

> You are sick and cannot go to work. What is your company's policy?

■ B. VALUED EMPLOYEES *The following are ten qualities often mentioned by managers as the qualities they are seeking in their employees. Match each quality with its definition.*

1. _____ Punctual

2. _____ Professional appearance

3. _____ Efficient

4. _____ Accurate

5. _____ Interacts well with coworkers

6. _____ Responsible

7. _____ Able to handle conflicts

8. _____ Good communications skills

9. _____ A team player

10. _____ Confident

a. Make few mistakes

b. Friendly with other workers

c. Can work well with a group

d. Speak and write well

e. Perform work quickly and well

f. Arrive on time

g. Believe in own ability

h. Dress neatly

i. Can take care of disagreements

j. Dependable

Choose three qualities that describe you as a worker. Explain to your group what you do at work and how these qualities apply to your job performance.

C. STUDENT TO STUDENT

Student A: *Turn to page 193. Read your partner questions 1 to 5.*
Student B: *Listen and write each question on the line above the correct answer.*

Jeff's Work Experience

1990	1991	1992	1993	1995	1996
Graduated from college	RepCo Repaired cars	ElCo Sold electrical appliances	Life Co Sold life insurance	Got married	CarCo Sells auto insurance

1. _____
   Since 1992.

2. _____
   No, he hasn't.

3. _____
   Since 1996.

4. Has Jeff ever sold life insurance? _____
   Yes, he has.

5. _____
   Four.

*Stop after number 5. **Student B** will turn to page 193 and read questions 6 to 10. **Student A** will look below and write each question above the correct answer.*

6. _____
   Yes, he is.

7. _____
   Since 1995.

8. _____
   In 1996.

9. _____
   Yes, he does.

10. _____
    Three times.

Practicing on Your Own

■ A. AN EVALUATION *Rewrite these sentences. Put the adverb or time expression in the correct place.*

1. Susan has worked overtime. (several times this month)

   Susan has worked overtime several times this month.

2. She has followed company policies. (always)

   _____

3. She has been rude to a customer. (never)

_____

4. We have received complaints about her. (rarely)

_____

5. She has made a mistake on a form. (from time to time)

_____

6. She has been late. (rarely)

_____

7. She has made helpful suggestions. (several times)

_____

8. She has been able to handle conflicts with customers. (usually)

_____

9. She has been able to solve problems. (usually)

_____

10. She has let her personal problems interfere with work. (from time to time)

_____

■ B. EVALUATION REPORTS
The owner of Excel Electronics is writing end-of-month evaluation reports on two of her employees. Karl is going to receive a promotion. David is going to lose his job. Using the present perfect tense, complete this chart comparing the two employees.

Karl

1. He has always arrived on time.

2. He has taken one sick day.

3. He has sold twenty-five televisions.

4. _____

David

1. David has been late ten times. _____

2. _____

   _____

3. _____

   _____

4. He has gotten into several arguments with customers.

5. _____

6. He has always written the correct

   address on delivery notices.

7. He has often worked overtime.

5. He has made mistakes on seven bills of sale.

6. _____

7. _____

■ C. TENSE CONTRAST *Complete these conversations with the verb in the correct tense. Use the present, past, future, or present perfect tense.*

1. **Manager**: We _advertised_ (advertise) for a tool-and-die maker last month, but we

   have only _received_ (receive) four applications.

   Boss: _____ you _____ (interview) any of them yet?

   Manager: Yes, all of them. One _____ (change) jobs five times in the

   last four years, so we _____ (negative—want) her. Another

   _____ (receive) several negative job evaluations. The third person

   _____ (negative—speak) any English. The last one

   _____ (negative—have) any job experience, but we might hire him.

2. **Nelson:** My brother, Jim, _____ (graduate) from college last month.

   George: What _____ he _____ (major) in?

   Nelson: Biology. He _____ (receive) three job offers so far.

   George: Three! Which one _____ he _____ (take)?

   Nelson: He _____ (decide) to take a job as a technician for a phar-

   maceutical company.

3. **Cheung:** My company _____ (lay off) five hundred employees two

   months ago!

   Hong: What are you going to do?

   Cheung: I _____ just _____ (accept) a job at a software com-

   pany in Austin, Texas. Actually, I _____ (make) more money than I

   _____ (do) at my old job.

Hong: How _____ your family _____ (feel) about moving to Texas?

Cheung: We _____ (fly) down there last month to look for an apartment. My wife _____ (fall) in love with the city.

Hong: Well, good luck to you.

Having Fun with the Language

■ **A. MY JOB** *Describe your job to your group or to the class. Include the following points. Your classmates can ask you more questions. (Note: In the United States and Canada, it is not polite to ask a person about his or her salary.)*

What company do you work for? What does this company do?

What is your title? What do you do?

What kind of education, training, or experience does a person need for your job?

Do you have any benefits?

Is there any possibility for advancement or promotion at your job?

Do you like your job? Why or why not?

Why would a person want your job? Why wouldn't a person want your job?

■ **B. JOB SEARCH** *The following are ways that people often find jobs. Have you ever tried any of these? Which ones do you think would be the most effective? How did you find your job? How did your friends or family find their jobs? Write two more suggestions on the lines.*

Look in the classified ads in the newspaper

Ask friends about jobs in their companies

See a sign on a store or a building

Go into a place of business and ask if there are any openings

Go to an employment agency

_____

_____

C. AN EVALUATION
Imagine that you are the boss or supervisor at your place of work. Use the vocabulary and expressions in this unit and write an evaluation of your job performance.

Grammar Summary

1. Usage

The present perfect tells about repeated actions in the past. These activities may continue or may be repeated in the future.

Place adverbs of frequency (e.g., *always, sometimes, often, never*) before the main verb:

He has **always** *arrived* on time.

He has **never** *had* a problem with a co-worker.

Time expressions (e.g., *from time to time, so far this month*) are usually at the end of a sentence. Sometimes we put time expressions at the beginning.

He has written 15 new policies **so far this month.**

He has attended training classes **from time to time.**

2. Questions with *ever*

Have you ever used a computer?	Yes, I have.
Has he ever had a job interview?	No, he hasn't.
Have they ever worked overtime?	Yes, they have.

At the Ball Game

Present Perfect Continuous

Vocabulary

fans

minor league

inning

score

pitcher

strike out

error

at the plate

cheering

concession stand

A. LISTEN: AT THE BALLPARK
Listen to a description of this minor league baseball game. Then read the statements below. Circle **T** *if the statement is true, or* **F** *if the statement is false.*

T   F   1. The home team is playing a team from the next town.

T   F   2. The fans have been watching the game for about an hour.

T   F   3. It's the fifth inning.

T   F   4. Angela has been selling tickets.

T   F   5. She has sold over 1,000 tickets.

T   F   6. The home team has been getting a lot of hits.

T   F   7. The fans have been buying a lot of hot dogs.

T   F   8. Stanley has been selling a lot of soda.

T   F   9. The fans have been sitting quietly, watching the game.

T   F   10. The home town team is winning.

B. *FOR OR SINCE*
Complete these sentences with **for** *or* **since***.*

Use **for** with an amount of time:	Use **since** to tell when an action started:
for an hour	**since** 5:00
for three hours	**since** the game began
for five days	**since** 1995

1. The fans have been watching this game _____ an hour.

2. The fans have been waiting for this game _____ a year.

3. They have been arguing about which team is better _____ fifty years.

4. Alberto has been pitching _____ an hour.

5. He has been standing in the hot sun _____ 2:00.

6. Alberto has been playing for this team only _____ May.

7. The fans have been sitting in the sun _____ over an hour.

8. Carmen and Fernando have been coming to games regularly _____ two months.

9. They have been buying Italian ices and soda _____ the game started.

10. Baseball has been popular in the United States _____ the mid-1800s.

> Check the two sentences that are correct.
> ❑ They began to play baseball an hour ago.
> ❑ They began to play baseball for an hour.
> ❑ They have been playing baseball an hour ago.
> ❑ They have been playing baseball for an hour.
> What's the difference between **an hour ago** and **for an hour**?

■ C. PRESENT PERFECT CONTINUOUS

Choose the correct verb from the list below and complete these sentences with the present perfect continuous tense.

play   strike   make
walk   sell   work
make   serve   call
throw

Present Perfect Continuous			
I			
You	have		
We	haven't		
They		been	watching the game.
He	has		
She	hasn't		
It			

1. Angela _____ tickets since 12:00.
2. The pitcher _____ out a lot of players.
3. The home team _____ a lot of errors.
4. An announcer _____ the game.
5. The pitcher _____ fast balls.
6. The people in the concession stand _____ hard.
7. Jason _____ Italian ices.
8. Mia and Ana _____ lemonade.
9. Stanley _____ up and down, selling sodas.
10. The teams _____ for an hour.

■ D. TENSE CONTRAST

Answer these questions about the ball game. Use the present, present continuous, the present perfect, or the present perfect continuous.

EXAMPLE

What is Stan doing?   He's selling soda.
How long has he been selling soda?   He's been selling soda for about two hours.
How many sodas has he sold?   He's sold a lot of sodas.

1. What is Angela doing?
2. How long has she been selling tickets?
3. How many tickets has she sold?
4. What is Alberto doing?
5. How long has he been pitching?
6. How many players has he struck out?
7. When did the baseball game begin? What time is it now?
8. How long have the teams been playing?
9. What is Jason doing?
10. How long has he been working today?

■ **A. BASEBALL** *Sit in a group of three or four students. In each group, be sure there are one or two students who are baseball fans. What do you know about baseball?*

1. Label these players on the diagram below.

   first baseman   right fielder   shortstop

   second baseman   center fielder   pitcher

   third baseman   left fielder   catcher

2. Where does the batter stand? Draw him in this picture.
3. How many innings are there in a baseball game?
4. How many strikes make an out?
5. Explain how the game is played.
6. Give two rules in baseball.
7. Name five major league baseball teams. Which team is in your state or area? Do you have a favorite team?
8. Can you name two baseball players? What positions do they play?

Is baseball popular in your country?

Are any of the rules different?

What is the most popular sport in your country?

■ B. A BUSY WEEKEND *There are three items in each group. What do you think each person has been doing?*

paint
easel   She's been painting a picture.
brushes

helmet	sleeping bags	shovel	cue stick
riding gloves	tent	seeds	fifteen balls
a tire repair kit	backpack	watering can	one cue ball
computer	ball	vacuum cleaner	suitcase
keyboard	bat	mop	passport
modem	glove	dust cloth	tickets

Now fill in each list with three related items that a person is using. Sit with another group and read your lists. Can the other students guess what each person has been doing?

1. _____ 1. _____ 1. _____

2. _____ 2. _____ 2. _____

3. _____ 3. _____ 3. _____

■ C. FACTS ABOUT MYSELF *Complete this information about yourself.*

1. I live in _____ . (city)

2. I work at _____ .

3. In my free time, I _____ .

4. I like to (play) _____ .

5. I study at _____ .

6. In order to stay healthy, I _____ .

7. I go to Dr. _____ . (dentist)

*Now read each fact about yourself to a partner. Your partner will ask you a **How long** question for each response.*

A: I live in Minneapolis.
B: How long have you been living here / there?
A: I've been living here for two years.

D. STUDENT TO STUDENT

Student A: *Turn to page 193.*
Student B: *Student A will ask you ten questions about the concession stand. Listen and circle the correct answer below.*

1. a. Yes, it is.   b. Yes, it does.   c. Yes, it has.

2. a. Yes, they are.   b. Yes, they do.   c. Yes, they have.

3. a. Yes, he is.   b. Yes, he does.   c. Yes, he has.

4. a. Yes, he is.   b. Yes, he does.   c. Yes, he has.

5. a. No, he isn't.   b. No, he doesn't.   c. No, he hasn't.

6. a. Yes, he is.   b. Yes, he does.   c. Yes, he has.

7. a. No, he isn't.   b. No, he doesn't.   c. No, he hasn't.

8. a. Yes, they are.   b. Yes, they do.   c. Yes, they have.

9. a. No, they aren't.   b. No, they don't.   c. No, they haven't.

10. a. Yes, they are.   b. Yes, they do.   c. Yes, they have.

*When you finish, **Student B** will read questions 1 to 10 on page 193. **Student A** will circle the correct answers above.*

Practicing on Your Own

■ A. PRESENT PERFECT AND PRESENT PERFECT CONTINUOUS *Read each sentence; then circle the sentence that is true.*

1. They've been playing baseball for two hours.

   a. They're still playing baseball.

   b. They played baseball for two hours, and the game is over.

2. People have been buying a lot of sodas.

   a. People are still buying sodas.

   b. People are not going to buy any more sodas.

3. He has watched many baseball games.

   a. He's watching a game now.

   b. He often watches baseball games and will probably continue to watch them.

4. She has drunk two sodas.

   a. She is drinking a soda now.

   b. She finished two sodas. She might drink another.

5. He has been working at the radio station for five years.

   a. He started to work at the radio station five years ago. He still works there.

   b. He left his job at the radio station after working there for five years.

6. The player has just hit a home run.

   a. The player hit a home run sometime during the game.

   b. The player hit a home run a short time ago.

7. Jason has been making Italian ices all afternoon.

   a. Jason can finally take it easy. He's finished working for the day.

   b. Jason is still busy making Italian ices.

8. The home team has been making a lot of errors.

   a. The home team made some errors during the game, but they won't make any more.

   b. The home team made some errors, and it's possible that they will make more.

B. CONVERSATIONS *Complete these conversations with the correct form of the verb in parentheses. Use the present continuous, past, present perfect, present perfect continuous, or future.*

1. **A:** How long _have_ you _been watching_ (watch) that game?

   B: About three hours. It's the ninth inning, and the score is 5-5.

   A: Who _____ (play)?

   B: The Mets and the Dodgers.

2. **A:** _____ they _____ (open) the ticket window yet?

   B: No, not yet.

   A: How long _____ you _____ (wait) in line?

   B: I _____ (get) here two hours ago.

3. **A:** Where's Ken? It's 5:00, and it's time to leave for the game.

   B: I don't know. I _____ (call) him three times, but I only get his

   machine.

   A: We _____ (wait) for him for an hour. We

   _____ (leave) now.

4. **A:** This traffic is terrible! We _____ (miss) the game.

   B: We _____ (sit) in traffic for an hour.

   A: We _____ (leave) the house two hours ago. Next

   time, I _____ (watch) the game on TV.

5. **A:** Mom, can I have another hot dog?

   B: David, you _____ already _____ (eat) two hot dogs!

   A: Can I have a soda?

   B: You _____ (have) two cans of soda! You _____ (get) sick!

   A: But, Mom, I'm thirsty.

   B: OK. That man _____ (sell) Italian ice. Buy one for each of us.

C. HOW LONG/HOW MANY *Write questions for each answer about the people in the pictures.*

1. What's she doing?

   She's riding her bicycle.

2. How long has she been riding her bicycle?

   For two hours.

3. How many miles has she ridden?

   Twenty miles.

4. _____?

   They're playing tennis.

5. _____?

   For an hour.

6. _____?

   Six games.

7. _____?

   He's running.

8. _____?

   For thirty minutes.

9. _____?

   Four miles.

10. _____?

    They're playing baseball.

11. _____?

    Since 6:00.

12. _____?

    Eight innings.

Having Fun with the Language

A. BASEBALL CARDS *Your teacher will bring a pack of baseball cards to class. Look at the players and answer these questions.*

Who is this player?

What team does he play for?

What position does he play?

How many different teams has he played for?

How many years has he been playing for his current team?

How many games has he played during his career?

What's his batting average? Does he bat righthanded or lefthanded?

How many home runs has he hit?

B. AN INTEREST OR A HOBBY *Bring in an item that represents one of your interests. In a small group, ask each other questions about your interests. For example, if you play tennis, bring in a can of tennis balls or a tennis magazine. The other students will ask questions, such as: How often do you play tennis? Where do you play? How long have you been playing tennis? Are you taking lessons?*

Grammar Summary

1. Usage

The present perfect continuous talks about an action that started in the past and continues into the present. The action is not yet complete.

2. Statements

I have been watching this game for three hours.

They **have been playing** baseball since 5:00.

The pitcher **has been throwing** fast balls.

3. Questions

Have you **been watching** the game?

Has she **been sitting** in the sun?

Have they **been selling** a lot of soda?

4. *How long/How many questions*

How long asks about an amount or length of time. We often use the present perfect continuous with *How long* questions.

How long has he been selling tickets?   Since 12:00.

How many asks about a number. We often use the present perfect with *How many* questions to show *How many so far* or *How many up to now.*

How many tickets has he sold?   About 800.

The American Dream

Infinitives

Grammar in Action

■ **A. THE AMERICAN DREAM** *Read this narrative about the American dream. Draw a box around each verb that is followed by an infinitive. Underline the infinitive.*

Infinitives			
Use an infinitive (**to** + verb) after the following verbs:			
agree	hate	love	seem
ask	hope	manage	try
(be) able to	intend	need	volunteer
can afford	know how	offer	want
decide	learn (how)	plan	wish
expect	like	refuse	would like

Jimmy Carter, former president of the United States, said that the United States has not become a melting pot, but a beautiful mosaic—different people, different beliefs, different hopes, different dreams. So, what is the American dream? It is the opportunity that we expect to have in order to find happiness. It is difficult to define happiness and success because people have different beliefs about what these qualities are. Many people hope to find happiness and success outside themselves. They think they will be able to find happiness when they are rich. Others hope to become famous. Some decide to pursue power. Then there are other people who seem to believe that happiness is found inside themselves. They would like to find inner peace. They wish to love and be loved. They want to serve the community and give back to the world some of what they have gotten. They believe Rabbi Heschel's words: "To be is a blessing. To live is holy."

B. LISTEN: PERSONAL DREAMS
Listen to each person talk about his or her dream.
After you listen to each person, complete the information below with an infinitive.

1. He expects his sons _____ well in school.

2. He encourages his boys _____ sports.

3. He wants _____ his sons to college.

4. It's difficult _____ money for college.

5. They've managed _____ a little money.

1. He has decided _____ a landscaping business.

2. He knows how _____ a new lawn.

3. He needs _____ a truck and lawn equipment.

4. His brother has offered _____ him money.

5. He has agreed _____ him back in four years.

6. He needs _____ at least thirty customers to start the business.

1. She would love _____ some more time for herself.

2. She would like _____ in the park every day.

3. She wants _____ some books.

4. She would like _____ on the phone with her friends.

5. Her daughter asked her _____ at her school.

■ C. VERB + INFINITIVE *Talk about your own plans, using the cues below.*

plan / study   I plan to study computer science.

1. plan / study
2. would like / find
3. decide / travel
4. want / see
5. expect / live

6. try / learn how
7. intend / buy
8. volunteer / help
9. need / save
10. hope / become

■ D. MY TEACHER *Ask your teacher these questions. They all contain infinitives.*

1. Why did you decide to become a teacher?
2. Have you learned how to speak another language?
3. Do you plan to get another degree?
4. Where would you like to travel?
5. Do you want to live in another country for a few years?
6. Do you know how to cook any ethnic food?
7. Do you expect to work here until retirement?
8. Will you remember to pass me at the end of this year?
9. Would you agree to end class early today?

> Think of two other questions with infinitives to ask your teacher.

■ E. VERB + OBJECT + INFINITIVE *Rewrite these words of advice to young people. Use the verb in parentheses.*

Verb + Object + Infinitive				
Use an object + an infinitive after the following verbs.				
advise	enable	help	persuade	tell
allow	encourage	hire	remind	urge
ask	expect	invite	require	want
convince	forbid	permit	teach	warn

My sister said, "Continue with your education." (convince)

My sister **convinced me to continue** with my education.

My sister **convinced me not to quit** school.

1. My mother said, "Learn to play an instrument." (encourage)
2. My brother said, "Don't do drugs." (warn)
3. My father said, "You must be home by midnight." (require)
4. My grandmother said, "Don't marry young." (advise)
5. My teacher said, "You should study two hours a day." (urge)
6. My best friend said, "Try out for the baseball team." (encourage)
7. My uncle said, "Don't drop out of high school." (persuade)
8. My aunt said, "Respect your parents." (tell)
9. My grandfather said, "Write to me once a month." (expect)
10. He also said, "Have faith, even in difficult times." (remind)

■ F. MY GOALS *Complete these sentences about your future goals.*

1. Next year, I plan _____ .

2. Three years from now, I expect _____ .

3. Five years from now, I hope _____ .

4. Ten years from now, I would like _____ .

Sit in a small group and read your goals. Your classmates will give you encouraging advice beginning with some of these phrases:

It's a good idea to…

It's going to be difficult to…

It's natural to…

It's idealistic to…

It might be helpful to…

It's smart to…

It's important to…

■ A. A HAPPY LIFE *What is necessary to have a happy and successful life? Put a check in the appropriate column below.*

	Very Important	Important	Not Very Important	Not Important
1. to be rich	❑	❑	❑	❑
2. to be famous	❑	❑	❑	❑
3. to have a job I love	❑	❑	❑	❑
4. to do things useful for society	❑	❑	❑	❑
5. to be healthy	❑	❑	❑	❑
6. to be a good parent	❑	❑	❑	❑
7. to have a happy marriage	❑	❑	❑	❑
8. to have good friends	❑	❑	❑	❑
9. to have a good education	❑	❑	❑	❑
10. to have free time	❑	❑	❑	❑
11. to have power and influence	❑	❑	❑	❑
12. to believe in God	❑	❑	❑	❑
13. to have inner peace	❑	❑	❑	❑
14. to speak English well	❑	❑	❑	❑
15. to own a house	❑	❑	❑	❑

Sit with a partner and discuss choices above. Then discuss these questions. Can your group reach a consensus on what makes a happy life?

1. What's important to you?
2. What's not important to you?
3. What do you think is easy?
4. What do you think is difficult?

B. THE TIMES OF OUR LIVES
These photos show four ages in a person's life. What are the differences at each stage? What can a person do? What are a person's hopes and plans and dreams? Using an infinitive, talk about each of these different ages with the verbs below.

baby

teenager

adult

senior citizen

EXAMPLE

Many teenagers want to own a car.

Some senior citizens like to volunteer in schools or hospitals.

Verb + Infinitive

(be) able	want	know how
hope	try	can't afford
like	expect	need

C. FAMILY ADVICE
What advice did your family give you when you were younger? Complete each of these sentences.

1. My mother said, "_____."

2. My father said, "_____."

3. My brother said, "_____."

4. My aunt said, "_____."

5. My grandmother said, "_____."

Now sit with a small group. Tell your classmates the advice your family gave you. Read each sentence, and then say it again using a verb from the box plus an infinitive.

advise
ask
encourage
expect
tell
warn

EXAMPLE

My mother said, "Write me every week."

My mother expected me to write her every week.

■■

D. STUDENT TO STUDENT *Having good friends is one component of a happy life.*
However, it is not easy to make good friends or to continue friendships.

Student A: *Turn to page 194.*

Student B: *Student A will read five statements about friends. Listen again and write three of the sentences that are true for you.*

1. _____

2. _____

3. _____

When you finish, change pages. **Student B** *will turn to page 194 and read five new sentences.* **Student A** *will write three of the sentences that are true for him or her.*

Practicing on Your Own

■ A. VERB + INFINITIVE *Complete the following sentences with infinitives.*

1. By next year, I hope _____ .

2. By the time I complete this course, I will know how _____ .

3. Before I take another course, I will need _____ .

4. When I speak English more fluently, I will be able _____ .

5. I plan _____ at the end of this course.

6. After I graduate from college, I would like _____ .

7. My teacher requires the students _____ .

8. When I have a better job, I expect _____ .

B. VERB + INFINITIVE
Write a sentence describing each person's dream. Use the following verbs:
hope, want, wish, plan, promise, would like.

1. _____

_____

2. _____

_____

3. _____

_____

4. _____

_____

5. _____

_____

6. _____

_____

■ C. VERB + OBJECT + INFINITIVE *Write each sentence again, using the verb in parentheses. You will need to change the wording in some of the sentences.*

1. When Luis came to the United States, his family thought he would make a lot of money. (expect)

   Luis's family expected him to make a lot of money.

2. My mother's dream was for me to become a doctor. (want)

   My mother wanted me to become a doctor.

3. Laura's father said that she should take dancing lessons. (encourage)

   _____

4. The boss signed a contract for John to manage the restaurant. (hire)

   _____

5. My mother showed me that I could be happy no matter what my circumstances were. (teach)

   _____

6. The consulate gave Taylan a visa to come to the United States. (permit)

   _____

7. My parents didn't let me study acting because they thought I wouldn't be able to find a job. (forbid)

   _____

8. When the boss didn't raise her salary, Mara's friends talked her into finding another job. (persuade)

   _____

9. My uncle gave me a loan so that I could go to college. (enable)

   _____

10. My teacher told me that I should study math in college. (advise)

    _____

11. My brother thought that I should become an artist. (tell)

    _____

Maya Angelou is a famous African American author, poet, playwright, director, performer, singer, and producer. She survived a very poor and painful childhood to achieve success in all of these fields. She even had the distinction of being invited by President Clinton to write and deliver a poem at his first Inauguration Day ceremony. She was the first African American and the first woman to have this honor. It was a difficult task for her to write a poem that would touch the millions of diverse people who would listen to her. Throughout her life, however, she was willing to accept all challenges as opportunities for personal growth and change. One of these challenges occurred when she was fifteen.

At that time, she decided to take some time off from school and get a job. She didn't want any of the jobs traditionally held by women. She longed to be a conductor on a San Francisco trolley car, but this was a difficult goal to achieve since African Americans were not permitted to work on the trolleys. Maya refused to accept this prejudice, and her mother encouraged her to fight.

Maya went to the trolley office for an interview, but the personnel manager refused to see her. She was determined not to give up, and she returned to that office every day for three weeks until he decided to see her. Finally, he asked her to fill out an application form, and he gave her an interview. She became the first African American woman conductor on a San Francisco trolley. To read more about Maya Angelou, read *I Know Why the Caged Bird Sings*.

> Underline all the verb + infinitive structures in this story.

1. What did President Clinton select Maya Angelou to do?
2. When did she decide to take a year off from school?
3. What did she want to be?
4. Why wasn't it easy for her to get a job as a trolley car conductor?
5. What was the personnel manager reluctant to do?
6. What was her mother's reaction?
7. What did Maya refuse to do?
8. What did she finally manage to accomplish?
9. What does this experience show us?

Write about someone in your family or someone you know who has overcome a difficult time in life. What happened at this time? How did this person cope with and survive the situation? If you are not revealing confidences, share the story with your classmates.

Sharing Our Stories

Read Manpreet's story about her hopes and dreams for her life in the United States.

My husband and I are from India, from the city of Ludhiana in the state of Punjab. We arrived in the United States in 1994. My husband had a degree from a university in India, but he wasn't able to find a job. We decided to come to the United States for the work opportunities here in this country. My husband came here first. He began to work in an Indian restaurant where he is now the manager. He saved money and then sent tickets for me and our little daughter. My husband likes his work and would like to start his own business someday, probably a restaurant.

I planned to be a doctor. I finished university and my residency and internship in India. But when I arrived here and submitted my transcripts, they told me that I needed to begin my education again. They only gave me credit for a small number of courses. I feel very disappointed, but I refuse to be discouraged. I have changed my major to nursing. I have already been accepted into a nursing program. When I finish my English courses, I intend to get my registered nurse degree.

My joy in life is our daughter, Roopsi, who is five years old and in kindergarten. She speaks English, but at home we speak Punjabi. I think it's important to maintain your native language with your children. We visit India every year or two and I want her to be able to speak with her cousins and grandparents. There is also a small Indian community in our town, so we can celebrate Indian festivals together. The families are friendly, and we call each other, babysit for each other, and we like to cook together on the weekends.

Manpreet Kaur, India

Having Fun with the Language

■ A. QUOTATIONS *Discuss the following quotations about happiness in a small group. What do they mean? Do you agree or disagree with them?*

1. *The greater part of our happiness or misery depends on our dispositions, and not our circumstances.* —Martha Washington

2. *It is neither wealth nor splendor, but tranquillity and occupation which give happiness.* —Thomas Jefferson

3. *The search for happiness is one of the chief sources of unhappiness.* —Eric Hoffer

4. *If you ever find happiness by hunting for it, you will find it, as the old woman did her lost spectacles [glasses], on her nose all the time.* —Josh Billings

B. SUCCESS *Read this poem by Ralph Waldo Emerson. Then add two more lines describing your definition of success.*

What is success?

To laugh often and much;

To win the respect of intelligent people and the affection of children;

To earn the appreciation of honest critics and endure the betrayal of false friends;

To appreciate beauty;

To find the best in others;

To leave the world a bit better, whether by a healthy child, a garden path or a redeemed
social condition;

To know even one life has breathed easier because you have lived;

That is to have succeeded.

Grammar Summary

1. Verb + infinitive

Use an infinitive (**to** + verb) after certain verbs. A list of verbs that are followed by an infinitive is in the appendix.

I expected **to find** a job easily.

I plan **to get** a degree in accounting.

2. Verb + object + infinitive

Use an object + infinitive after certain verbs. A list of verbs that are followed by an object + infinitive is in the appendix.

My brother persuaded *me to come* to the United States.

I told *him to send* me a ticket.

3. The infinitive after adjectives

When a verb follows an adjective, use the infinitive form. A list of adjectives that are followed by an infinitive is in the appendix.

It was *difficult to accomplish* my goals.

4. The infinitive as subject

If an infinitive begins a sentence, it is the subject of the sentence.

To find the best in others is success.

12 Immigration

Gerunds

A. GERUNDS: ELLIS ISLAND *Read this paragraph about Ellis Island. In the story, there are nine gerunds (verb + **ing**). Five of the gerunds are underlined. Find the other four gerunds and underline them.*

140

On Sunday, September 9, 1990, the Ellis Island Museum in New York Harbor was dedicated as a memorial to the more than twelve million people who came through Ellis Island from 1892 to 1924. The island was the entry point for ships from all over the world, especially Europe. Immigrants risked <u>losing</u> everything they owned to come to America, the land of opportunity. They dreamed about <u>coming</u> to the United States to find freedom from hunger, religious persecution, and political problems. After <u>leaving</u> their homes behind, they boarded overcrowded ships to begin the long voyage, often under unhealthy and uncomfortable conditions. However, they continued <u>believing</u> in their dreams and anticipated <u>finding</u> a land of unlimited opportunities. As the ships approached New York Harbor, immigration officials stopped the boats, and ferries brought the new arrivals to Ellis Island. After checking their bags, the immigrants had to have a medical check. Everyone was afraid of taking this exam because the people who failed it were prevented from entering the United States. Then, as they waited on long benches, they worried about answering questions when it came their turn to see the legal inspectors. After the immigrants spent about five hours on Ellis Island, immigration officials approved the entry of healthy arrivals and gave them the long-awaited card with the word "ADMITTED."

Verb + Gerund

Use a gerund (verb + *ing*) after the following verbs:

They **hated** *taking* the medical exam.

admit	discuss	keep on	recommend
anticipate	dislike	like	regret
appreciate	don't mind	love	resent
avoid	enjoy	miss	resist
can't help	finish	postpone	start
continue	give up	practice	stop
consider	hate	quit	suggest
delay	imagine	recall	understand

■ B. EARLY IMMIGRANTS
Read these sentences about the story. Change the words in parentheses to the gerund form.

In the early 1900s, immigrants started (come) to the United States in record numbers.
In the early 1900s, immigrants **started** *coming* to the United States in record numbers.

1. People discussed (leave) their countries for many months or years before making the journey.
2. They anticipated (provide) a better life for their children.
3. They imagined (live) in a country of freedom and of plenty.
4. The new immigrants couldn't help (worry) about money and work.
5. They hated (spend) long weeks on the overcrowded ships.
6. They continued (believe) in their dreams even though the voyage was difficult.
7. Some couples postponed (get) married until one of them had a job in America.
8. Some of the immigrants regretted (leave) their countries.
9. Most of the arrivals succeeded in (enter) the country.
10. They looked forward to (start) their lives in a new land.

■ C. RESTATEMENT
Restate these sentences in your own words. Use the verb in parentheses plus a gerund. Some statements are negative. (See Grammar Summary.)

My father thought I should come to the United States to get a better education. (recommend)
My father **recommended** *coming* to the United States to get a better education.

1. I wondered whether I should wait until I finished university in my country. (consider)
2. I didn't make my decision for nearly two months. (postpone)
3. I told everyone that I wasn't afraid to leave my country. (deny)
4. The consulate said to submit an application for a visa as soon as possible. (recommend)
5. If I waited too long I might not get the visa on time. (risk)
6. I didn't like to make all the arrangements by myself. (resent)

7. I was sorry that I didn't say good-bye to my friends at work. (regret)

8. I liked the flight to America. (enjoy)

9. I knew that life in America would be difficult. (understand)

10. I am sad that I can't see my family and friends. (miss)

Verb + Preposition + Gerund

Use a gerund (verb + *ing*) after the following verbs + prepositions:

Immigrants **planned on** *working* hard.

adjust to	complain about	interested in	succeed in
approve of	count on	keep on	suspect of
argue about	depend on	look forward to	talk about
believe in	dream about	object to	think about
blame for	forget about	plan on	warn about
care about	insist on	prevent from	worry about

Be + Adjective Phrase + Gerund

Use a gerund (verb + *ing*) after the following: *be* + adjective phrase.

Antonio was in favor of coming to America, but his wife wasn't.

afraid of	fond of	in favor of	proud of
capable of	good at	interested in	tired of
famous for	guilty of	opposed to	upset about

■ D. VERB OR ADJECTIVE PHRASE + GERUND *Complete these sentences about your-self by using a gerund. Then read your sentences to a partner.*

Before coming to the United States...

1. I dreamed about _____ .

2. I planned on _____ .

3. I looked forward to _____ .

4. I worried about _____ .

5. I was interested in _____ .

After coming to the United States...

6. I am proud of _____ .

7. I have adjusted to _____ .

8. I often complain about _____ .

9. I think about _____ .

10. I'm capable of _____ .

E. LISTEN: THE FIRST YEAR
Listen to each person talk about his or her decision to come to the United States and the first year in this country. Answer the questions below. Many include a gerund or an infinitive.

1. What did she worry about before coming to the United States?
2. What did her brother encourage her to do?
3. What does she regret?
4. What did she need to do when she went to the store?
5. How is her English now?
6. What will she continue doing?

1. What was he concerned about?
2. Why was he able to find a job easily?
3. What does he admit?
4. What did he dream about having?
5. Where did he want to go?
6. What can he afford to do?
7. What doesn't he mind doing?

1. What did he have a hard time adjusting to?
2. What does he hate wearing?
3. Why did he have difficulty getting around?
4. What does he miss the most?
5. What does he miss seeing?
6. What does he plan on doing when he returns to his country?

F. PREPOSITIONS: CITIZENSHIP
*Use a gerund after the prepositions **before** and **after**.*

Preposition + Gerund
Use a gerund (verb + **ing**) after these prepositions:
After *studying* the citizenship book, she easily passed the test.

after	besides	in addition to	without
before	by	instead of	

EXAMPLE

Before I applied for citizenship, I lived here for five years.

Before *applying* for citizenship, I lived here for five years.

1. After I obtained the application for naturalization, I had my fingerprints taken.
2. After I filled out the application, I wrote the check.
3. Before I sent in the paperwork, I had the required photographs taken.
4. After I sent in the papers, I waited a long time.
5. While I waited, I studied for the citizenship test.
6. Before I took the oath of allegiance, I took and passed the citizenship test.
7. After I took the oath of allegiance, I was a citizen.

■ G. CONTRAST: GERUND OR INFINITIVE *Do you use a gerund or an infinitive after these verbs? Read the sentence again and use the correct form of the word in parentheses.*

1. It was impossible (find) a job in my country.
2. I miss (see) my friends from my country.
3. I intend (visit) my native country next year.
4. I expect my cousin (arrive) soon.
5. Have you ever considered (become) a citizen?
6. How long do you plan (stay) in this country?
7. How long do you plan on (stay) in this country?
8. My parents appreciate (receive) a check from me each month.
9. She's proud of (start) her own import business.
10. I promised (write) my grandparents often.
11. Besides (have) difficulty finding a job when I first arrived, I didn't like (live) with my uncle.
12. He enjoys (read) books on American history.
13. My uncle refused (change) his long name when he became a citizen.
14. Sometimes I regret (come) to this country.
15. I sometimes complain about (live) here, but then I recall the reasons that I came.

Working Together

A. PLANS *Sit in a small group. Use the verbs in the box below to talk about your preparations to come to America. All these verbs must be followed by gerunds. You might want to use some of phrases below the box to help you recall your plans.*

begin	start	continue	keep on
finish	stop	quit	regret

apply	work	learn (English)
save (money)	contact (relatives)	make (arrangements)
live	fill out	shop
take	buy	call
find out	write	

EXAMPLE

A: I began learning English. How about you?

B: No, I didn't study English. I regret not taking classes.

A: I continued working until the week before I left.

B: Me, too. I couldn't quit working.

B. FEELINGS *What do you like about the United States? What don't you like? Write two or three things in each column below.*

like enjoy	don't mind	dislike / don't like	can't stand
ordering take-out food		wearing a winter coat	

Sit in a small group of three or four students. Compare your charts and discuss the similarities and differences.

EXAMPLE

A: I can't stand wearing a winter coat and hat and gloves.

B: Why?

A: I come from a tropical country. I don't like heavy clothing.

C. I AGREE/I DISAGREE
Seven commonly discussed issues are listed below. Use the verbs in the box, all requiring gerunds, and state your opinion about each. Give your reasons.

1. Limiting new immigration
2. Mandating English only in government offices
3. Restricting the sale of handguns
4. Prohibiting the sale of automatic weapons
5. Increasing the tax on cigarettes
6. Allowing prayer in public schools
7. Placing more restrictions on teenage driving

Verb + Preposition + Gerund
(be) against
(be) in favor of
(be) opposed to
agree with
approve of
disagree with
object to
worry about

D. STUDENT TO STUDENT

Student A: Turn to page 194.
Student B: Student A will begin to read a list of gerund phrases. Write the phrase in the column that describes your experience in adjusting to life in this country. Stop when you have three phrases in each column. You do not need to use every phrase.

This was easy for me:	This was difficult for me
1. _____	1. _____
2. _____	2. _____
3. _____	3. _____

When you finish, change pages. **Student B** *will turn to page 194.* **Student A** *will write the phrases in the columns that describe his or her experience.*

Practicing on Your Own

A. CONTRAST: GERUND OR INFINITIVE
Some of these verbs take the infinitive; others take the gerund. Complete these sentences with the correct form of the word in parentheses.

1. I didn't know how ___to speak___ (speak) English when I came to the United States.

2. I have made a lot of progress in _____ (learn) English.

3. At first, I tried _____ (translate) every word.

4. I was nervous about _____ (talk).

5. I was afraid of _____ (make) a mistake.

6. I felt like _____ (cry) when people didn't understand my pronunciation.

7. _____ (listen) to a new language is very difficult.

8. I practiced _____ (speak) in my own bedroom with the door closed.

9. My teacher told us not _____ (memorize) separate words, but to learn new words in a sentence.

10. He encouraged us _____ (talk) to our neighbors and co-workers.

11. He also urged us _____ (read) at least thirty minutes a day.

12. In addition to _____ (learn) the language, you must also learn cultural differences.

13. _____ (nod) your head up and down means "yes" in this country, whereas it means "no" in my native country.

14. It took time to adjust to _____ (call) my teacher by his first name.

15. Here, the teacher expects us _____ (look) her in the eye when we speak.

16. It is impolite _____ (ask) people their age or income or weight.

17. _____ (learn) a language is a process that takes a lifetime.

■ B. COMPLETE *Carlos came to the United States two years ago. Use your imagination to complete these sentences about his experience with the correct infinitive or gerund form.*

Carlos hated his first six months in the United States.

1. Carlos _hated not understanding when people spoke to him_____.

2. He missed _seeing his family and friends_____.

3. He complained about _____.

4. Finally, his brother persuaded him _____.

So, Carlos enrolled in an English as a second language program.

5. Carlos began _____.

6. He found he was good at _____.

7. His teacher encouraged him _____.

8. He was determined _____.

Two years later, Carlos now has a job he likes and has made a few friends.

9. He is no longer worried about _____.

10. He enjoys _____.

11. He has adjusted to _____.

12. He's looking forward to _____.

■ C. RESTATEMENT *Ana wrote about her experience coming to the United States. Rewrite each sentence using the verb in parentheses with an infinitive or a gerund.*

1. I couldn't go to college in my country because my family didn't have enough money. (be able)

    I wasn't able to go to college in my country. _____

2. We sold our house in order to have enough money to come here. (need)

    _____

3. My husband came here first. (decide)

    _____

4. He was going to send for me in one year. (expect)

    _____

5. I didn't want to stay behind. (opposed to)

    _____

6. I lived with my brother and sister-in-law, but I wasn't happy there. (upset about)

    _____

7. At my husband's advice, I enrolled in English classes in my country. (urge)

    _____

8. My husband and I didn't see one another for three years. (miss)

    _____

9. Right now, I speak well but my writing is weak. (need)

    _____

10. When my English is stronger, I will study accounting. (plan on)

    _____

■ D. TIME LINE
Complete these sentences about Jarek. Use a gerund and the related information from the time line.

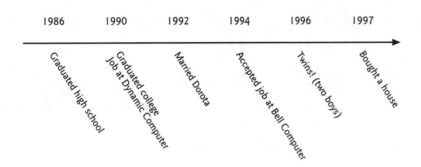

| 1986 | 1990 | 1992 | 1994 | 1996 | 1997 |

Graduated high school

Graduated college
Job at Dynamic Computer

Married Dorota

Accepted job at Bell Computer

Twins! (two boys)

Bought a house

1. In addition to ___attending college___ , Jarek worked part time from 1986 to 1990.

2. After _____ , Jarek found a good job.

3. Instead of _____ after college, Jarek waited for two years.

4. Before _____ , Dorota worked full time.

5. After _____ , she quit work to take care of them.

6. Before _____ , Dorota and Jarek lived in an apartment.

Sharing Our Stories

Read Robin's story about his grandmother's experience coming to the United States.

Maria Amantea was born in an obscure town in Calabria, Italy, on January 27, 1888. Her father was a poliziotto, a policeman. He was grateful for having this job because it was good, steady work, but it kept him away from home most of the time. Maria's mother was left by herself with her four children. Life was difficult for her, as she worried about raising her four children on her own. Because Maria was the oldest daughter, she was responsible for taking care of the younger children and helping with the housework.

When Maria was seven years old, her mother died. Even though Maria was very young, she now had the full responsibility for taking care of the children and the house. It was very hard work. Sometimes she cried because she missed being with her mother. Sometimes she cried because she detested doing all of the housework by herself.

Soon Maria's father remarried, but her new mother was the stereotypical stepmother. She resented having to take care of another woman's children. She was mean to them and often hit them for no reason. Maria and her brothers were upset and sad about living under those terrible conditions.

When Maria was seventeen, her father brought Salvatore home to meet his daughter. She was quite nervous about meeting him since she had never dated. Three days later, they were married. Maria was afraid of getting married because she really didn't know Salvatore and she certainly didn't love him. However, as they walked down the aisle of the small church, she didn't realize that she would one day be grateful to her father for introducing them. She would grow to love him—a love that would last a lifetime.

At that time, there were very few jobs in Italy. Salvatore was worried about not having a job, so he, like a lot of other young men, decided to go to America to find work. He entered the United States at Ellis Island, and then went to Pennsylvania to work in a coal mine. The separation was difficult for both Maria and him, so after saving enough money, he returned to Italy to take Maria back to America with him.

They were excited about going to America, the land of opportunities and dreams. By the time they boarded the ship headed for America, Maria was pregnant. They arrived in New York, went through Ellis Island and settled in San Antonio, Texas. With the money Salvatore had saved, he bought a horse and cart and sold fruits and vegetables. Salvatore was good at doing business and he was able to make good money there. In 1925, after having several children, they decided to move to New Jersey to be close to Maria's sister and brothers. They settled in Paterson, where Salvatore succeeded in finding a job in the silk industry. He remained at this job until he retired many years later.

Robin Cannata, the United States

Underline the gerunds in this story. (Hint: There are eighteen gerunds.)

 Write about your experience coming to the United States. Dates, details, and feelings will help make your story interesting and personal.

Having Fun with the Language

A. PACKING *What did you bring with you when you came to the United States? What did you leave in your country that you wanted to bring here? Make two lists and discuss them with your classmates. What items appear on several lists?*

I packed:	I couldn't take:

B. CITIZENSHIP TEST *Before you take the Citizenship test, the INS gives you a list of one hundred questions that you can study to prepare for the test. Ten of the questions are on the left. Match them with the answers on the right.*

1. How many stars are there on the flag?
2. How many stripes are there on the flag?
3. Who elects the president of the U.S.?
4. What is the Constitution?
5. What are the three branches of government?
6. How many senators are there in Congress?
7. Why did the Pilgrims come to America?
8. What is the national anthem of the U.S.?
9. Which president is called "Father of our Country"?
10. Name one benefit of being a citizen of the U.S.

a. The electoral college.
b. The supreme law of the land.
c. For religious freedom.
d. Fifty.
e. The Star Spangled Banner.
f. Thirteen.
g. Legislative, executive, and judicial.
h. One hundred.
i. You can get a federal government job.
j. George Washington.

Grammar Summary: Gerunds

▪ 1. Verb + gerund

Use a gerund (simple verb + *ing*) after certain verbs. A list of verbs that are followed by a gerund is in the appendix.

They **discussed** *coming* to the United States.

She **regretted** *leaving* her parents and sisters.

She regretted **not saying** good-bye to her friends.

He resents **not having** more free time.

▪ 2. Verb + preposition + gerund

Use a gerund (simple verb + *ing*) after most verb phrases with a verb and a preposition. A list of verbs + prepositions that are followed by a gerund is in the appendix.

He **worried about** *finding* a job.

They are **planning on** *living* with relatives for the first year.

▪ 3. *Be* + adjective phrase + gerund

Use a gerund (simple verb + *ing*) after the verb *be* + adjective phrase. A list of the adjective phrases that are followed by a gerund is in the appendix.

She is **in favor of** *becoming* a citizen.

He is **proud of** *passing* his English proficiency test.

▪ 4. Preposition + gerund

Use a gerund (simple verb + *ing*) after most prepositions. A list of common prepositions which are followed by a gerund is in the appendix.

Before *leaving* Japan, Hiro visited his grandparents.

▪ 5. Gerund as subject

A gerund (simple verb + *ing*) can be the subject of a sentence.

Leaving his native country was difficult for Boris.

Learning English was easy for my children.

13 Business and Industry

Present Passive

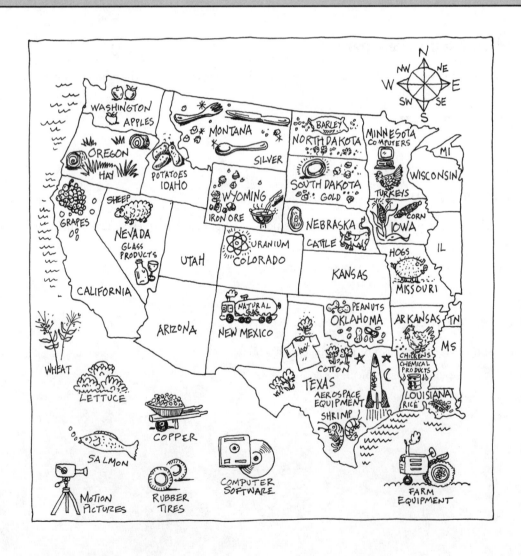

◼ A. MAP STUDY *Look at this map of the western half of the United States and answer the questions.*

1. Find California. Which state is located north of California?

2. Find Kansas. Which state is located west of Kansas?

3. Find South Dakota. Which state is located north of South Dakota?

4. Find Arizona. Which state is located east of Arizona?

5. Find Montana. Which state is located south of Montana?

6. Find Minnesota. Which state is located south of Minnesota?

7. Find New Mexico. Which state is located north of New Mexico?

8. Find Arkansas. Which state is located west of Arkansas?

9. Find Utah. Which state is located south of Utah?

10. Find Nebraska. Which state is located east of Nebraska?

◼ B. PRODUCT MAP *Look at the product map. If the sentence is true, circle **T**. If it is false, circle **F**.*

T	F	1.	Grapes are grown in California.
T	F	2.	Silver is mined in Montana.
T	F	3.	Potatoes are grown in New Mexico.
T	F	4.	Peanuts are grown in Oklahoma.
T	F	5.	Turkeys are raised in Utah.
T	F	6.	Gold is mined in Iowa.
T	F	7.	Cattle are raised in Nebraska.
T	F	8.	Rice is grown in Louisiana.
T	F	9.	Grapes are grown in Minnesota.
T	F	10.	Hogs are raised in Missouri.

Participles
catch—caught
design—designed
grow—grown
manufacture—manufactured
mine—mined
produce—produced
raise—raised

C. LISTEN: A PRODUCT MAP *Look at the products on the bottom of page 154. Listen to the information about each product. Draw a line from the product to the state. When you finish, try to retell the information about each product.*

Passive Voice			
Form the present passive with ***be*** + a participle.			
Computer equipment	is	manufactured	in (state).
Rubber tires	are		

■ D. QUESTIONS *Ask and answer questions about each of the products below.*

EXAMPLE

Is wheat grown in Kansas?   Yes, it is.

Where is wheat grown?   In Kansas.

■ E. ACTIVE OR PASSIVE? *Circle the correct form of the verb.*

> **Active and Passive**
> Active: **Farmers** grow corn in Iowa.
>   In the active, the subject performs the action.
> Passive: **Corn** is grown in Iowa.
>   In the passive, the product is emphasized.

1. Farmers   **grow   are grown**   corn in Texas.
2. Gold   **mines   is mined**   in South Dakota.
3. Ranchers   **raise   are raised**   cattle in Nebraska.
4. Workers   **mine   are mined**   uranium in Nebraska.
5. Turkeys   **raise   are raised**   in Minnesota.
6. Farmers   **grow   are grown**   lettuce in Arizona.
7. Iron ore   **mines   is mined**   in Wyoming.
8. Ranchers   **raise   are raised**   hogs in Missouri.
9. Farmers   **grow   are grown**   apples in Washington.
10. Rice   **is grown   are grown**   in Louisiana.

156

Working Together

A. WELL-KNOWN COMPANIES
Match the product in the lefthand column with the name of the company in the righthand column. Which company manufactures or produces each product?

> **EXAMPLE**
>
> Telephones are manufactured by AT&T.

telephones	Gerber
jeans	Avon
baby food	AT&T
cosmetics	IBM
computers	Levi Strauss
oil	General Electric
appliances	Gillette
bandages	Exxon
razors	Xerox
copiers	Johnson and Johnson

> What are five products that you use in your home?
> By which company is each product made or manufactured?

B. DESCRIBING A PROCESS
Sit in a group. Use the pictures below and describe how orange juice is produced. Then write a short description of the process.

Vocabulary
pick—picked
take—taken
put—put
wash—washed
cut—cut
squeeze—squeezed
filter—filtered
transport—transported

■ C. OUR STATE

Work together in a small group. Draw the outline of your state on a large piece of paper. Answer these questions and mark the following places and items on your feature map.

1. What is the state capital? Where is it located on your map? Put a star next to the name of the capital.
2. What city are you in now? Place it on the map. Name three major cities in your state. Place them on the map.
3. What is the largest airport near your city? Show it on the map.
4. Write in the bordering states and oceans. How many states is your state bordered by?
5. Draw in two or three major rivers in blue. Name them.
6. Locate any national parks that are located in your state.
7. Indicate two major highways that travel through your state.
8. What farm products are grown in your state?
9. What major industries are located here?
10. How are goods transported into and out of your state?

Practicing on Your Own

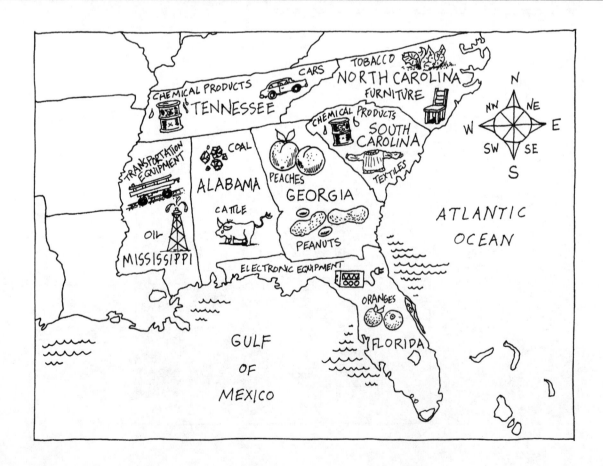

■ A. PRODUCT MAP *Complete these sentences about the products on this map, using the verbs below.*

grow   make   raise   manufacture   mine

1. Oranges _are grown in Florida._

2. Cars _____ .

3. Tobacco _____ .

4. Transportation equipment _____ .

5. Furniture _____ .

6. Peaches _____ .

7. Cattle _____ .

■ B. QUESTIONS *Complete these questions and answers about the product map.*

1. _Are_____ airplanes _manufactured_____ in Florida? _No, they aren't._____

2. _____ iron ore _____ in North Carolina?

   _____ .

3. _____ oil _____ in Mississippi? _____ .

4. _____ grapes _____ in Alabama?

   _____ .

5. _____ electronic equipment _____ in Florida?

   _____ .

6. Where _____ ? In South Carolina.

7. Where _____ ? In Alabama.

8. Where _____ ? In Tennessee.

9. What _____ ? Peanuts are.

10. What _____ ? Tobacco is.

■ C. WINE *Complete this story about wine production. Some verbs are active; others are passive.*

Wine is a light alcoholic beverage made from grapes. In many countries, it __is served__
(serve) with the evening meal or it _____ (use) in cooking. People often
_____ (celebrate) special occasions with a fine bottle of wine.

Two states, California and New York, _____ (produce) most of the wine
that _____ (come) from the United States. The wine grapes
_____ (grow) in vineyards. As the grapes ripen, they
_____ (check) carefully to determine the right time for picking, usually in
the late summer or early fall.

After the grapes _____ (pick), they _____ (crush)
mechanically. Some home wine makers still _____ (crush) grapes the
old-fashioned way, by foot. The natural wine yeast on the grape skin
_____ (ferment) the wine, changing the grape sugar into alcohol and
carbon dioxide. The juice from the grapes _____ (pump) into tanks, where
the fermentation process _____ (continue). White wine
_____ (ferment) without the skins; red wine _____
(ferment) with the skins.

After fermentation, the wine _____ (age) in storage tanks. Fine wine
_____ (age) in small oak barrels for up to nine months. Table wine
_____ (age) in large steel tanks for a much shorter time, often just a
few weeks. Finally, the wine _____ (pour) into bottles, and the workers
_____ (store) them in a cool, dark place.

The two most popular wines for meal time are red and white. Red wine
_____ (have) a stronger flavor. It _____ (serve) at
room temperature with heavier foods, such as beef, spaghetti, or spicy food. White wine
_____ (serve) chilled with lighter meals, such as chicken or fish.

Answer these questions about wine production.

1. When is wine served in your house?

   _____

2. What weather is best for excellent wine?

   _____

3. Is all wine made by wine-producing companies?

   _____

4. What does *ferment* mean?

   _____

5. Why is there a difference in the color of wine?

   _____

6. Which is aged longer, fine wine or table wine?

   _____

7. What kind of wine is served with turkey?

   _____

8. Which wine is best when it's served cold?

   _____

D. BUSINESS
The following information is from Hoover's Handbook of American Business, 1996. *Complete the questions below. Some are active; others are passive.*

Name of company: Wendy's	**Year established: 1969**

Headquarters: Dublin, Ohio

President: R. David Thomas   Pay: $1,287,227

Sample products: Big Bacon Classic, chicken club sandwich, stuffed baked potatoes

Number of restaurants: 6,262   Number of employees: 47,000

Key competitors: McDonald's, Pepsico, Subway, Boston Chicken, Domino's Pizza

Goal: Open 8,000 restaurants by the year 2,002; add more overseas restaurants.

Interesting fact: Thomas named Wendy's after his eight-year-old daughter.

Reprinted with permission from *Hoover's Handbook of American Business 1997*, copyright 1996 Hoover's, Inc., Austin, Texas, 800-486-8666.

1. What _is the name of this company_____ ?   Wendy's.

2. Where _____ ?   In Ohio.

3. When _____ ?   In 1969.

4. Who _____ ?   R. David Thomas.

5. How much _____ ? $1,287,227.

6. How many restaurants _____ ?   6,262.

7. How many people _____ ?   47,000.

8. What company _____ ?   McDonald's.

9. What _____ ?   To open more restaurants.

10. Who _____ ?   Thomas' daughter.

Having Fun with the Language

A. CLASS PRESENTATION
Use the encyclopedia, CD-ROM collection, or other resource in the school or local library. Research the process involved in making a product such as coffee, tea bags, paper, etc. Describe the process to the class.

■ B. COMPANY PROFILE

The Hoover *guides provide two-page descriptions of both national and international companies, including the name of a company, location, history, company president and salary, number of workers, and products. Choose a product that you own and look up the company in one of the Hoover guides, found in any public library. Complete the chart and make a short presentation to your class.*

Name of company:	**Year established:**

Headquarters: _____

President: _____ Pay: _____

Sample products: _____

Number of employees: _____

Key competitors: _____

Goal: _____

Interesting fact: _____

Grammar Summary

■ 1. Active and Passive

Active: *Farmers grow* grapes in California.
Passive: *Grapes are grown* (by farmers) in California.

In an active sentence, the subject performs the action (farmers).
In a passive sentence, the product, the action, or the process is emphasized (grapes). Use **by** to show the agent.

■ 2. Uses

a. We use the passive to emphasize the product, the action, or the process.

   Oranges **are transported** to processing plants.

b. We use the passive when the person who performed the action is unknown or understood.

   The wine **is delivered** to the restaurant every week. (unknown)
   White wine **is served** with chicken. (understood)

c. We can use the passive for general statements of fact.

   Fine wine **is aged** longer than table wine.
   Red wine **is fermented** with the skins.

■ 3. Questions

Cotton **is grown** in Texas.	**Is** cotton **grown** in Texas?	Yes, it is.
Grapes **are grown** in California.	Where **are** grapes **grown?**	In California.

14 Technology and Progress

Passive—Contrast

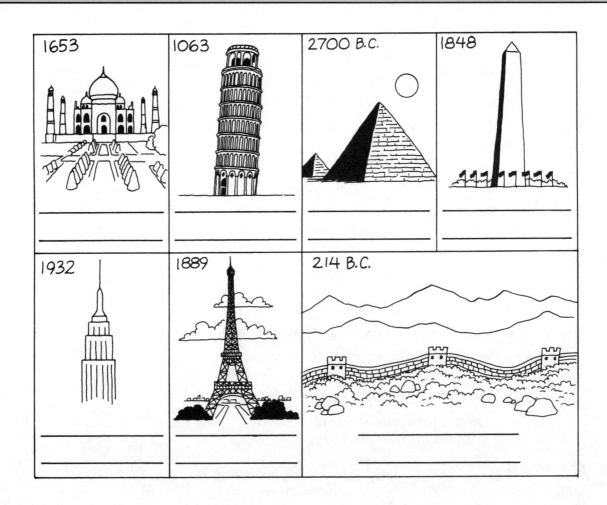

■ A. STRUCTURES *Write the structure and the country under each picture.*

Structure	Country
the Great Wall	the United States
the Washington Monument	Egypt
the Empire State Building	Italy
the pyramids	China
the Leaning Tower of Pisa	France
the Taj Mahal	the United States
the Eiffel Tower	India

■ B. STRUCTURAL FACTS *Read each fact. Which structure do you think it describes?*

EXAMPLE

They were used as tombs for Egyptian kings.

The pyramids.

Past Passive		
It	was	built.
They	were	

1. They are located on the Nile River.

2. It was built to protect China from its enemies, the Mongols.

3. This structure was built to honor the one-hundreth anniversary of the French Revolution.

4. It was constructed as a bell tower.

5. It was constructed by the king to honor his wife, Mumtaz Mahal.

6. It was built to honor the first president of the United States.

7. All parts of this iron structure were pre-made, then put together like a puzzle.

8. It is used as an office building.

9. It is surrounded by beautiful pools and gardens.

10. These structures are made of stone.

C. LISTEN: FAMOUS STRUCTURES
Listen to these descriptions of three of the structures in the pictures. Complete the chart with short notes; then answer the questions.

Structure	Purpose	Facts		Vocabulary
the pyramids Egypt				tombs
				buried
the Taj Mahal India				spirit
				slaves
				emperor
the Eiffel Tower France				dome
				erected
				exhibition
				puzzle

1. Where are the pyramids located?
2. What were they used as?
3. What did the Egyptians believe about death?
4. What is the largest pyramid called?
5. How long did it take to build this pyramid?
6. Where is the Taj Mahal located?
7. Why was it built?
8. What does the structure look like?
9. Where is the Eiffel Tower located?
10. Why was it built?
11. What material is it made of?
12. Was it constructed in Paris?

D. ACTIVE OR PASSIVE? *Circle the correct verb in each sentence.*

1. The pyramids **built**   **were built**   by slaves.

2. Slaves **built**   **were built**   the pyramids.

3. The Egyptian kings **used**   **were used**   the pyramids as tombs.

4. The pyramids **used**   **were used**   as tombs.

5. The Taj Mahal **surrounds**   **is surrounded**   by beautiful pools and gardens.

6. Beautiful pools and gardens **surround**   **is surrounded**   the Taj Mahal.

7. The Eiffel Tower **erected**   **was erected**   in Paris.

8. Workers **erected**   **was erected**   the Eiffel Tower in Paris.

9. The Eiffel Tower **constructed**   **was constructed**   of iron.

10. Workers **constructed**   **was constructed**   the Eiffel Tower of iron.

> What is the most famous structure in your country?
> Where is it located? When was it built? Why was it built?

E. FUTURE PASSIVE *Read each of these predictions made in 1995 about computer technology. What is the reality today?*

> **Future Passive**
> Most business **will be conducted** by computer.

EXAMPLE

Prediction: More mail will be sent by computer.

Today: I e-mail my family in Japan. It's free, and it's fast.

1. All new homes and buildings will be wired for computers.
2. All new cars will be equipped with computer "maps."
3. Home lights will be turned off and on automatically by home computer.
4. Most home TVs will be connected to the computer.
5. Most banking will be done on computer.
6. Twenty percent of all shopping will be conducted on the computer.
7. Most classrooms will be equipped with computers.
8. New employees will be expected to know how to use a computer.
9. Microsoft will still be recognized as the leader in computer technology.
10. Bill Gates will still be ranked as the richest man in America.

F. ACTIVE TO PASSIVE *Change the sentences below from active to passive. In several sentences, the agent is understood.*

> **Passive**
> Passive statements use a form of *be* and the past participle.
> | | |
> |---|---|
> | Present | The building **is made** of marble. |
> | Present Continuous | The building **is being painted**. |
> | Past | The building **was completed** in 1995. |
> | Future | The renovations **will be completed** next year. |
> | Present Perfect | The plans **have been approved**. |
> | Modals | The bridge **should be repaired** soon. |

EXAMPLE

On some highways, machines **are collecting** tolls electronically.

On some highways, tolls **are being collected** electronically.

1. Workers erected the first traffic light in London, England, in 1868.
2. People operated it by hand.
3. Fifty percent of U.S. drivers wear seat belts.
4. The law requires drivers to wear seat belts.
5. Seat belts have saved many lives.
6. The police use radar to catch speeders.
7. Many drivers install radar detectors.
8. Engineers are developing new types of speed detectors.
9. The police officer is going to catch the driver.
10. The police officer will charge him with speeding.

Working Together

■ A. FAMOUS INVENTIONS
Try to match the inventions below with the year and the inventor.
*Talk about each using **invent, develop,** or **discover**. The answers are on page 173.*

Invention	Year	Inventor
	1450	Gutenberg
	1609	Galileo
	1876	Bell
	1877	Edison
	1879	Benz
	1888	Eastman
	1903	Wright Brothers
	1906	Birdseye
	1927	Warner Brothers
	1938	Dupont
	1982	Jarvick
	1995	Microsoft

light bulb	hand-held camera	airplane
telescope	talking movies	Windows 95
printing press	telephone	Teflon
frozen food process	automobile engine	artificial heart

■ B. INVENTIONS THAT CHANGED THE WORLD
What was life like before we had five of the inventions in the list above? Write five more sentences.

> **EXAMPLE**
>
> Before the light bulb was invented, people read by candle or gas light.
>
> Before the frozen food process was developed, people canned fruits and vegetables.

C. STUDENT TO STUDENT

Student A: *Turn to page 195. Read the list of inventions and discoveries to* **Student B.**

Student B: *Look at the categories below.* **Student A** *will read a list of inventions and discoveries to you. Write each item in the correct category.*

_____ and _____ are used to send information.	_____ and _____ are used to see objects more clearly.	_____ and _____ are used to record and play back sounds.
_____ and _____ are used to see inside the body.	_____ and _____ are used to relieve pain.	_____ and _____ are used to warn or protect people.

When you finish, **Student B** *will turn to page 195 and read a second list.* **Student A** *will write the items in the correct categories above.*

Practicing on Your Own

■ **A. PASSIVE** *Complete these sentences in the passive. The verbs are in different tenses.*

1. Early people believed that disease _____ (cause) by evil spirits.

2. People _____ (cure) by a medicine man.

3. Hippocrates _____ (know) as the Father of Medicine.

4. Hospitals _____ (begin) by the Romans.

5. Today, hospitals _____ (locate) in all major cities.

6. The University of Pennsylvania School of Medicine _____ (establish)

   in 1765 as the first medical college in the United States.

7. Infections _____ (cause) by bacteria.

8. Before an operation, all equipment _____ (must / sterilize).

9. Penicillin _____ by Sir Alexander Fleming. (discover)

10. At present, new drugs _____ to treat infection. (develop)

11. New drugs _____ (discover) in the future.

12. Many advances _____ (made) in the treatment of AIDS.

■ **B. READING** *Read and complete this story about advances in heart procedures.   Some of the verbs are active; others are passive. Choose the correct verb tense.*

Heart disease is the number-one cause of death in the United States. For years, doctors _____ (develop) tests, medications, devices, and procedures to help patients with heart problems. But, when all else _____ (fail), a heart transplant may be necessary.

On December 3, 1967, in Capetown, South Africa, Dr. Christian Barnard _____ (perform) the first heart transplant. The heart of an auto accident victim _____ (transplant) into the body of Louis Washansky, a fifty-five-year-old man. He _____ (live) for eighteen days following the operation.

Since that day, over 15,000 heart transplants _____ (perform). The major difficulty in these procedures _____ (be) the rejection of the new heart by the body's immune system. In 1969, an anti-rejection drug, cyclosporine, _____ (discover) by Jean-Francois Borel. Today, heart transplants _____ (perform) throughout the world.

The first artificial heart _____ (implant) in Dr. Barney Clark in 1982. This heart _____ (name) the Jarvick-7 after its inventor, Dr. Robert Jarvick. Dr. Clark _____ (live) for 112 days. The next patient _____ (survive) 620 days. But research with the artificial heart _____ (discontinue). In 1990, approval for the Jarvick-7 _____ (recall) by the Food and Drug Administration.

Write questions for the answers below.

1. _____ _____ ? Dr. Christian Barnard.
2. _____ ? 18 days.
3. _____ ? By Jean-Francois Borel.
4. _____ ? In 1982.
5. _____ ? The Jarvick-7.
6. _____ ? In 1990.

■ C. ACTIVE TO PASSIVE *Change the sentences below from active to passive. In several sentences, the agent is understood.*

1. A doctor uses a stethoscope to examine a patient's chest.

   _____

2. The nurse places a thermometer under the patient's tongue.

   _____

3. The nurse takes blood from a vein in the patient's arm.

   _____

4. Blood banks test all blood.

   _____

5. Bernard Fantus established the first blood bank in the United States in Chicago, Illinois, in 1937.

   _____

6. Blood transfusions have saved many lives.

   _____

7. The kidneys remove poisonous wastes from the blood.

   _____

8. Dialysis machines can remove poisonous wastes from the blood.

   _____

9. Since 1973, the FDA has required childproof packaging for all medications.

   _____

10. The Chinese developed acupuncture.

    _____

11. The Chinese have used acupuncture for hundreds of years.

    _____

12. The doctor inserts fine needles at certain points under the skin.

    _____

Having Fun with the Language

A. OUTSTANDING ACHIEVEMENTS
Listed below are six outstanding achievements that were discovered or developed in the last twenty-five years. List two more. Talk about each achievement. What is it? What is it used for? Has your life been influenced by this development? Do you know anything about its development?

space satellites for communication   CAT scans   genetic testing

personal computer   MRIs   lasers

_____

_____

Grammar Summary

1. Active and Passive

Active: The doctor **performed** the operation.

Passive: The operation **was performed** by the doctor.

In an active sentence, the subject performs the action (the doctor).

In a passive sentence, the process, the product, or the action is emphasized (the operation). Use **by** to show the agent.

2. Uses

    a. We use the passive to emphasize the receiver of the action.

       The artificial heart **was developed** by Dr. Robert Jarvick.

    b. We use the passive when the person who performed the action is unknown or understood.

       The operation **was performed** yesterday.

    c. We can use the passive for general statements of fact.

       Blood **is composed** of millions of cells.

◼ 3. Passive statements

Passive statements use a form of *be* and the past participle.

Present	The building **is made of** marble.
Present Continuous	The building **is being painted.**
Past	The building **was completed** in 1995.
Future	The renovations **will be completed** next year.
Present Perfect	The plans **have been approved.**
Modals	The train station **may be completed** by next year.

◼ 4. *Wh* questions

Where **is** the Taj Mahal **located?**	In India.
When **was** it **built?**	In 1631.
When **will** the building **be renovated?**	Next year.

Answers to Working Together Exercise A (page 168)

Gutenberg—printing press; Galileo—telescope; Bell—telephone; Edison—light bulb; Benz—automobile engine; Eastman—hand-held camera; Wright brothers—airplane; Birdseye—frozen food process; Warner Brothers—talking pictures; Dupont—Teflon; Jarvick—artifical heart; Microsoft—Windows 95

15 Country Music

Adjective Clauses

Grammar in Action

■ A. WHO CLAUSES

The people in the picture are in Nashville, Tennessee, at the International Country Music Fan Fair, which has run for more than twenty-five years. It is a time for people who love country music to see and hear some of their favorite country artists perform. Fans can take photographs, get autographs, and buy memorabilia. The fair, which lasts for six days, is an annual event. Look at the picture and write the number of the comments below in the correct speech bubble. Then describe the person, using an adjective clause.

1. Are you going to buy those boots?
2. How many tickets do you want?
3. I'm your biggest fan.
4. It's over there.
5. I bought two tickets.
6. How many CDs did you buy?
7. Sure, I'll sign it.
8. This is our 20th Fan Fair.
9. How long have you been here?

EXAMPLE

The man <u>who is pointing to the shopping bag</u> is asking, "How many CDs did you buy?"
The man <u>who is standing on line</u> is asking, "How long have you been here?"

Complete these sentences about the picture by using an adjective clause.

1. The man who _____ is saying,

   "Are you going to buy those boots?"

2. The couple who _____ is saying,

   "This is our 20th Fan Fair."

3. The man who _____ is saying,

   "Sure, I'll sign it."

4. The man who _____ is asking,

   "How many tickets do you want?"

5. The man who _____ is saying,

   "I bought two tickets."

6. The woman who _____ is saying,

   "I'm your biggest fan."

7. The man who _____ is saying,

   "It's over there."

> Describe several students in your class, using an adjective clause.
> The man **who is sitting next to the door** came to class late.

B. LISTEN: COUNTRY MUSIC *Listen to the history of country music. Then circle **T** for true, or **F** for false.*

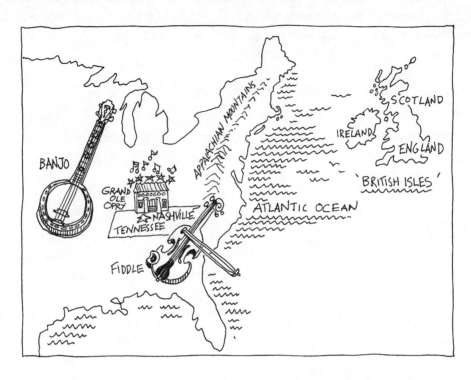

T	F	1. Today's country music originated in the British Isles.
T	F	2. The people from Appalachia sang all the time.
T	F	3. People sang to make their work go more slowly.
T	F	4. Country music, which the Appalachian people sang, was very complicated.
T	F	5. The banjo, which became popular among country musicians, came from South America.
T	F	6. The fiddle is the main instrument of country music.
T	F	7. The first superstars of country music recorded in 1947.
T	F	8. The Carter Family and Jimmy Rodgers, who both sang country music, became the first superstars of country music.

■ C. ADJECTIVE CLAUSES *Underline the adjective clause in the sentences below. Circle the relative pronoun and draw an arrow to the noun it modifies.*

> **EXAMPLE**
>
> The music, (which) is called country music, came from the British Isles.

Note:			
who	replaces a person	**whose**	replaces a possessive
whom	replaces an indirect object	**where**	replaces a place
which	replaces a thing	**when**	replaces a time

1. The people who immigrated to this country moved to land similar to their native land.
2. Today's country music began in the Appalachian mountains, which extend from the northeast to the south.
3. The music, which was very simple, was sung all the time.
4. The people who migrated from the British Isles brought their music with them.
5. The fiddler, whose instrument was the main country music instrument until the 1930s, made people dance.
6. The fiddler, whom the community considered a very important person, was necessary in every band.
7. The five-string banjo came from Africa, where it was used to play a different kind of music.
8. Jimmy Rodgers and the Carter family, whom a Virginia record company first recorded, were the earliest superstars of country music.

◼ D. RELATIVE PRONOUNS *Fill in the correct relative pronoun from the list below.*

who   which   whom   whose

1. Reba McEntire, _____ was country music's 1995 entertainer of the year, makes more money on her concerts than any other country star.

2. Reba McEntire, _____ songs are about independent women, has taken charge of her own career.

3. McEntire, _____ was forced to sound less country and more mainstream, was not popular for the first thirteen years of her career.

4. McEntire's first husband, _____ she divorced in 1987, did not promote her career well.

5. In 1982, McEntire had her first hit song, _____ was titled *"Can't Even Get the Blues."*

6. McEntire, _____ decided to become an opening act, gained confidence and became more popular after she took control of her career.

7. Her performances, _____ attract thousands of fans, cost a lot of money to organize.

8. McEntire's fans, to _____ she often talks after shows, are at least 50% male.

E. LISTEN: *WHEN AND WHERE AS RELATIVE PRONOUNS* *Listen to the information on the tape about singer Mary Chapin Carpenter and fill in the missing information in the sentences below.*

EXAMPLE

_1986_ was the year when _Mary Chapin Carpenter won five WAMMYs_ (Washington Area Musician's Awards).

In Washington, _where she moved after graduation,_ she wrote many original songs.

1. Tokyo is the city where _____.

2. Connecticut is the state where _____.

3. She attended Brown University, where _____.

4. After 1981, when she _____, she played at coffeehouses and clubs.

5. _____ is the city where she _____ by a recording studio executive.

6. _____ is the year when _____.

7. _____ is the year when _____ her first Grammy award.

Working Together

■ A. MUSICAL PREFERENCES *Complete the following sentences about your musical preferences.*

1. _____ is my favorite musician.

2. _____ is my favorite type of music.

3. _____ is my favorite musical group.

4. _____ is my favorite American singer/musician.

5. _____ is my favorite radio station.

6. _____ is my favorite place to go dancing.

Now rewrite your preferences using adjective clauses.

1. _____ , who is my favorite musician, is from

_____ .
        (country)

2. _____ , which is popular in _____ , is my
                                                          (country)

favorite music.

3. _____ , which is my favorite musical group, plays

_____ music.
        (type of music)

4. _____ , whose music is _____ , is my favorite
                                                         (adjective)

American singer/musician.

5. _____ , which is at _____ FM/AM, is my favorite radio station.
   (name of station)   (number)

6. _____ , which is located in _____ ,
        (city)

is my favorite place to go dancing.

Read your sentences to your group and compare preferences.

■ B. FIND SOMEONE WHO... *In a group of four or five students, answer the following questions about the members of your group. Then write an answer with a **who** clause.*

Who is a student who plays a musical instrument?

Sung Kul, **who is in a band**, plays the guitar.

Sung Kul, **who plays the guitar**, likes rock music.

1. Who is a student who plays a musical instrument?
2. Who is a student who listens to a Walkman®?
3. Who is the student who has been in the United States the longest?
4. Who is the student who has the longest hair?
5. Who is the student who studies the most?
6. Who is the student who is late to class most often?
7. Who is the student who is the most talkative?

Write three more questions to ask to other groups or classmates.

■ C. GETTING INFORMATION ABOUT THE AREA *Complete the questions. Then ask a partner your questions. How helpful was your partner?*

Do you know a music store where ___I can buy a CD by Reba McEntire?___

Yes, you should try the CD Den. It's on Broad Street.

1. Do you know a music store where _____?
2. Do you know a music school where _____?
3. Do you know a movie theater where _____?
4. Do you know a dance club where _____?
5. Do you know a restaurant where _____?
6. Do you know a supermarket where _____?
7. Do you know an auto repair shop where _____?

D. STUDENT TO STUDENT

Student A: Look at the sentences below.
Student B: Turn to page 195.
In each sentence, you both have different information about the same musician, singer, or composer.
Listen to each other carefully. Together, try to write a new, longer sentence about each person using an adjective clause.

Student A:

1. Elvis Presley sang and acted in movies.
2. Beethoven played in public at the age of seven.
3. The Beatles caused a sensation when they came to America.
4. Duke Ellington was a famous jazz composer.
5. Madonna has changed her appearance many times.
6. Janet Jackson became a star after she left her family's management.

Practicing on Your Own

■ A. RELATIVE PRONOUNS *Circle the correct relative pronoun.*

1. Nashville, **who   which   whom**   is located in Tennessee, is known as Music City.

2. For many years, the headquarters of country music has been Nashville, **when   where   which**   many of the singers live.

3. Two music producers, Owen Bradley and Chet Atkins, created the Nashville Sound, **whom   which   where**   was a more popular and sophisticated sound.

4. Chet Atkins, **whom   who   which**   some people say is the most recorded solo artist, built a billion-dollar business and recording center.

5. The idea of the Nashville sound was born **which   when   where**   Bradley and Atkins wanted to compete with more popular music.

6. 16th Avenue, **which   where   when**   a popular country radio station was started, is today called Music Row.

7. After World War II, **which** **where** **when** people needed some entertainment, the Grand Ole Opry recruited talent to perform country music.

8. Patsy Cline, **which** **whose** **whom** producer was Owen Bradley, became one of the most talented Nashville stars.

■ B. SENTENCE COMBINING *Read each pair of sentences. Then combine them into one longer sentence with an adjective clause. Use* **who** *or* **whose**.

1. Garth Brooks borrowed ideas from rock and roll. Garth Brooks's concerts often sell out.

   Garth Brooks, whose concerts often sell out, borrowed ideas from rock and roll.

2. Johnny Cash is one of the most famous country singers. Johnny Cash likes to wear black.
3. Patsy Cline died young. Patsy Cline sang the song "Crazy."
4. Reba McEntire manages her own company. Reba McEntire's ex-husband used to be her manager.
5. Wynonna has been singing solo for years. Wynonna used to sing with her mother.
6. Mary Chapin Carpenter is not a typical country star. Mary Chapin Carpenter's career began with folk music.
7. Lyle Lovett has also acted in a few movies. Lyle Lovett used to be married to Julia Roberts.
8. Roy Rogers performed with his wife, Dale Evans. Roy Rogers' television show was very popular.
9. Bill Ray Cyrus made country line dancing popular. Billy Ray Cyrus sang "Achy Breaky Heart."

■ C. MORE SENTENCE COMBINING *Read each pair of sentences. Then combine them into one longer sentence with an adjective clause. Use* **which, whom, where,** *or* **when**.

1. John Lennon became a successful solo artist after leaving the Beatles. Paul McCartney wrote many popular songs with him.

   John Lennon, with whom Paul McCartney wrote many popular songs, became a successful

   solo artist after leaving the Beatles.

2. Patsy Cline sang the song "Crazy." "Crazy" was written by Willie Nelson.
3. The Beatles toured all over Europe and America. In America, they had many devoted fans.
4. John Lennon died in 1980. In 1980, John Lennon was assassinated by a fan.
5. For a long time, karaoke singing has been popular in Asia. In Asia, high school students, university students, and business people all enjoy karaoke.
6. Pavoratti is a famous tenor. Many other artists have performed with Pavoratti.

7. The five-string banjo was first used in Africa. The five-string banjo became a popular country music instrument.

8. Disco music was popularized in the late 1970s. In the late 1970s, the movie *Saturday Night Fever* was a big hit.

9. Seiji Ozawa worked with many other orchestras before he joined the Boston Symphony. The Boston Symphony Orchestra appointed him conductor in 1973.

Having Fun with the Language

A. COUNTRY MUSIC *Your teacher is going to play a few country music songs. Listen, and give your opinion of the music. Do you like the song? Why or why not? Can you understand any of the lyrics? What is the song about?*

B. MINI-PRESENTATION *Choose a popular musician from your country. Select one of the artist's songs. Write down one of the verses in the original language of the song and then in English. Play the song for your classmates. Explain why you have chosen the artist and the song.*

C. VISIT A MUSIC STORE *Visit a local music store. Go to the country music section and find recordings by one of the following artists:*

Reba McEntire	Garth Brooks
Mary Chapin Carpenter	Johnny Cash
Shania Twain	Lyle Lovett

Report to a group of classmates with the following information:

a. How many recordings did you find?
b. What's the most recent recording by this singer?
c. Is one of the recordings a *live* recording?
d. What other recordings did you look at while you were in the store?
e. Did you buy anything? If so, what did you buy?

Grammar Summary

■ 1. Adjective clauses

An adjective clause describes a noun. It can describe a subject or an object.

■ 2. *Who* and *Which* clauses

Who and *Which* can replace a subject.

a. The man is singing a song. (The man) who is wearing a cowboy hat.

   The **man** <u>who is wearing a cowboy hat</u> is singing a song.

b. Country music is very popular. (Country music) which started in the Appalachian mountains.

   Country music, **which** <u>started in the Appalachian mountains</u>, is very popular.

■ 3. *Whom* and *Which* clauses

Whom (Who) and *Which* can replace an object.

Whom (Who) is often used with a preposition. *Whom* is more formal than *Who.*

a. Reba McEntire controls her own business. Many people admire (Reba McEntire.) whom

   Reba McEntire, **whom** <u>many people admire</u>, controls her own business.

b. The banjo was one of the first instruments in country music bands. African slaves brought (the banjo) which from Africa.

   The banjo, **which** <u>African slaves brought from Africa</u>, was one of the first instruments in country music bands.

■ 4. *Whose* clauses

Whose shows possession. It replaces possessive nouns and pronouns.

   Garth Brooks always plays to sold-out audiences. (Garth Brooks') whose latest song was a hit.

   Garth Brooks, **whose** <u>latest song was a hit</u>, always plays to sold-out audiences.

 # Appendix

Verb + Gerund

Use a gerund (verb + *ing*) after the following verbs:

admit	discuss	keep on	recommend
anticipate	dislike	like	regret
appreciate	don't mind	love	resent
avoid	enjoy	miss	resist
can't help	finish	postpone	stop
continue	give up	practice	start
consider	hate	quit	suggest
delay	imagine	recall	understand

Verb + Preposition + Gerund

Use a gerund (verb + *ing*) after the following verbs + prepositions:

adjust to	complain about	interested in	succeed in
approve of	count on	keep on	suspect of
argue about	depend on	look forward to	talk about
believe in	dream about	object to	think about
blame for	forget about	plan on	warn about
care about	insist on	prevent from	worry about

Be + Adjective Phrase + Gerund

Use a gerund (verb + *ing*) after the following: *be* + adjective phrase.

afraid of	famous for	guilty of	proud of
ashamed of	fond of	in favor of	tired of
capable of	good at	opposed to	upset about

Preposition + Gerund

Use a gerund (verb + *ing*) after these prepositions:

after	besides	in addition to	without
before	by	instead of	

Infinitives

Use an infinitive (*to* + verb) after the following verbs:

agree	forget	manage	remember
ask	hate	need	seem
(be) able to	hope	offer	try
can afford	intend	plan	volunteer
choose	know how	prefer	wait
decide	like	prepare	want
expect	learn (how)	promise	wish
fail	love	refuse	would like

Verb + Object + Infinitive

Use an object + an infinitive after the following verbs:

advise	encourage	help	permit	tell
allow	expect	hire	persuade	want
ask	forbid	instruct	remind	warn
convince	force	invite	require	urge
enable	get	need	teach	

Adjective + Infinitive

Use the infinitive form after adjectives such as these:

ambitious	easy	horrible	logical	realistic
bad	foolish	idealistic	lonely	sad
courageous	fun	important	naive	selfish
creative	good	intelligent	natural	terrible
dangerous	healthy	interesting	polite	thoughtful
difficult	helpful	kind	reasonable	wonderful

Verbs

Simple Form	Simple Past	Past Participle
be	was / were	been
bear	bore	born
become	became	become
begin	began	begun
bite	bit	bitten
break	broke	broken
bring	brought	brought
build	built	built
buy	bought	bought
catch	caught	caught
choose	chose	chosen
come	came	come
cost	cost	cost
cut	cut	cut
do	did	done
draw	drew	drawn
drink	drank	drunk
drive	drove	driven
eat	ate	eaten
fall	fell	fallen
feed	fed	fed
feel	felt	felt
fight	fought	fought
find	found	found
fit	fit	fit
fly	flew	flown
forget	forgot	forgotten
get	got	gotten
give	gave	given
go	went	gone
grow	grew	grown
hang	hung	hung
have	had	had
hear	heard	heard
hit	hit	hit
hold	held	held
hurt	hurt	hurt
keep	kept	kept
know	knew	known
lay	laid	laid

Simple Form	Simple Past	Past Participle
leave	left	left
let	let	let
lie	lay	lain
lose	lost	lost
make	made	made
meet	met	met
pay	paid	paid
put	put	put
quit	quit	quit
read	read	read
ride	rode	ridden
ring	rang	rung
run	ran	run
say	said	said
see	saw	seen
sell	sold	sold
send	sent	sent
set	set	set
sing	sang	sung
sit	sat	sat
sleep	slept	slept
speak	spoke	spoken
speed	sped	sped
spend	spent	spent
stand	stood	stood
stick	stuck	stuck
sting	stung	stung
strike	struck	struck
swim	swam	swum
take	took	taken
teach	taught	taught
tell	told	told
think	thought	thought
throw	threw	thrown
understand	understood	understood
wake	woke	waken
wear	wore	worn
win	won	won
write	wrote	written

Student to Student Exercises

Unit 1, page 14, Student A

Student A and *Student B* both have information about Marisa's schedule. *Read your statements to each other, but do not look at one another's books. Can you figure out Marisa's schedule?*

Student A:

1. Marisa takes American history after she takes English.
2. Marisa eats lunch at 11:00.
3. Marisa doesn't take a foreign language in the morning.

Unit 2, page 28

Student B: Your partner will ask you five questions. Choose the correct answer below and read it to your partner. Your partner will write the answer.

    a. They wrote letters.

    b. Benjamin Franklin did.

    c. They became popular after the mid 1700s.

    d. Because land transportation was slow and difficult.

    e. Men on horses carried the letters and messages.

When you finish, change pages. **Student B** *will turn to page 28.*

Student A: Listen and choose the correct answer below. Read it to your partner.

    f. They helped build houses and barns.

    g. They liked to watch horse racing.

    h. Yes, they did. Cats and dogs were popular.

    i. They went to taverns.

    j. They often lasted several days.

Unit 1, page 14, Student B

Student A and *Student B* both have information about Marisa's schedule. *Read your statements to each other, but do not look at one another's books. Can you figure out Marisa's schedule?*

Student B:

1. Marisa plays volleyball after homeroom.
2. Marisa takes biology two hours before she eats lunch.
3. Marisa goes to English after she eats lunch.

Unit 3, page 43, Student A

Student A: You each have a short sentence. **Student A** *will read his or sentence, then* **Student B** *will read his or her sentence for the same number. Combine the sentences with a future time clause using* **before** *or* **after**. *Write the five new sentences on page 43. Remember to use pronouns for repeated names.*

Student A:

1. Pete is going to propose to Lydia.
2. Pete is going to ask Lydia to marry him.
3. Pete and Lydia are going to get engaged.
4. Pete and Lydia are going to finish college.
5. Pete and Lydia are going to get married.

Unit 6, page 81, Student A

You each have information about five different people or places. Read your sentences about each person or situation. Put the information together and make a logical conclusion about each person or situation. Write your conclusion with **must**.

Student A:

1. Elena had a small salad for lunch.
2. Armin isn't in class today. He's in bed.
3. We have to get Alex to the hospital immediately.
4. That restaurant opened just last month.
5. New Jersey is one of the smallest states.
6. Kyoko keeps a calendar of all her appointments and meetings.

Unit 5, page 67

Student A: *Turn to page 67.*
Student B: *Student A will ask you four questions about Canada. Listen and give the correct answer. Then write the question. Be careful! The questions are not in order.*

_____

It's 6,416 kilometers (3,987 miles) long.

_____

English and French.

_____

The Arctic, the Pacific, and the Atlantic.

_____

No, it isn't. It's the second largest.

*Now ask **Student A** each question below. Listen carefully and write the answers.*

5. The capital of Canada is Vancouver, isn't it?

_____

6. What percentage of the population speaks English?

_____

7. Do most immigrants settle in Vancouver?

_____

8. What are the three largest cities in Canada?

_____

Unit 3, page 43, Student B

Student B: You each have a short sentence. **Student A** *will read his or sentence, then* **Student B** *will read his or her sentence for the same number. Combine the sentences with a future time clause using* **before** *or* **after**. *Write the five new sentences on page 43. Remember to use pronouns for repeated names.*

Student B:

1. Pete is going to buy an engagement ring.
2. Pete is going to talk to Lydia's father.
3. Lydia is going to call her mother.
4. Pete and Lydia are going to get married.
5. Pete and Lydia are going to go on a honeymoon.

Unit 6, page 81, Student B

You each have information about five different people or places. Read your sentences about each person or situation. Put the information together and make a logical conclusion about each person or situation. Write your conclusion with **must**.

Student B:

1. Elena has a booklet in her purse called *The Calorie Counter*.
2. There's a thermometer and a bottle of aspirin on Armin's dresser.
3. Alex was just stung by a bee.
4. People have to wait over an hour for a table.
5. New Jersey has one of the largest populations in the United States.
6. Everything on Kyoko's desk in order.

Unit 8, page 103

Student A: Turn to page 103.
Student B: Read the information below to **Student A.**

Student B:

1. George and Barney moved to Boston in 1995, and they still live there.
2. Maria used to live in Chicago. She moved to Miami when she got married.
3. Ricardo arrived in this country two years ago. He's still here.
4. We want to see that movie, but we've been very busy lately.
5. My mother got a cough three weeks ago, and she can't seem to get over it.

Now, change pages. **Student A** *will read the information below (6 to 10.)* **Student B** *will complete the sentences.*

Student A:

6. I saw my brother two years ago, but not since then.
7. Henry had a heart attack; then he had kidney trouble. I think he's out of the hospital.

8. Amy is almost ready to leave. She has her plane ticket. She is looking for her passport.

9. Sara began to work at the post office four years ago.

10. I first met Thomas five years ago.

Unit 9, page 112

Student A: *Read your partner questions 1 to 5 below*
Student B: *Turn to page 113. Listen and write each question you hear on the line above the correct answer.*

1. Has Jeff ever sold life insurance?
2. How many companies has Jeff worked for?
3. Has Jeff ever sold automobiles?
4. How long has Jeff sold car insurance?
5. How long has Jeff been a salesperson?

Stop after number 5. **Student A** *will turn to page 113.* **Student B** *will read questions 6 to 10 below.*

6. How many times has Jeff changed jobs?
7. Does Jeff sell car insurance?
8. When did he leave Lifeco?
9. Is Jeff married?
10. How long has Jeff been married?

Unit 10, page 123

Student A: *Read questions 1 to 10 below, under* **Student A.** *Are your partner's answers correct?*
Student B: *Turn to page 123.*

Student A:

1. Is it hot?
2. Are the fans hot?
3. Does Jason own the concession stand?
4. Has Jason been making Italian ices?
5. Does Jason get a lot of tips?
6. Has Jason made a lot of money today?
7. Has Jason taken a break?
8. Are Mia and Ana friends?
9. Have they been watching the game?
10. Have the fans been buying a lot of soda?

Student B

1. Is it a Sunday afternoon?
2. Are people thirsty?
3. Is Jason busy today?
4. Is Jason making Italian ices?
5. Has Jason been watching the game?
6. Does Jason work hard?
7. Is Jason selling tickets?
8. Do Mia and Ana always work together?
9. Have they been talking together?
10. Are the fans cheering their home team?

When you finish, change pages. **Student B** *will ask questions 1 to 10 above, under* **Student B,** *and check the answers.* **Student A** *will turn to page 123.*

Unit 11, page 134

Having good friends is one component of a happy life. However, it is not easy to make good friends or to continue friendships.
Student A: *Read* **Student B** *the five statements below about friends.*
Student B: *Turn to page 134.*

Student A:

1. It is easy for me to make friends.
2. I am reluctant to talk at a party to people I don't know.
3. I am afraid to call people on the telephone.
4. I am careful not to talk about personal matters when I first meet someone.
5. It's difficult to maintain my relationships with friends in my native country.

When you finish, change pages. **Student A** *will turn to page 134.*

Student B:

1. I am eager to begin conversations with people I don't know well.
2. I am determined to keep my long-term relationships.
3. I am willing to help my friends.
4. I am more likely to make friends at school than at a party.
5. It's important to have a best friend.

Unit 12, page 147

Student A: *Read the gerund phrases in column 1 to* **Student B.** *Stop when your partner has three phrases in each column.*
Student B: *Turn to page 147.*

Student A:	Student B
Learning English	Learning English
Finding a job	Meeting new friends
Talking on the telephone	Wearing different clothes
Adjusting to the weather	Not living with my family
Getting used to American food	Understanding the news
Reading the newspaper	Banking
Living in an apartment	Living in a city
Shopping in American stores	Understanding food labels

When you finish, change pages. **Student A** *will turn to page 147.* **Student B** *will read the phrases in the right-hand column.*

Unit 14, page 169

*Student A: Read this list of inventions and discoveries to **Student B**.*
Student B: Turn to page 169.

Student A:

e-mail	airbags	CAT scans	answering machines
compact discs	contact lenses	yoga	radar
aspirin	the Internet	telescope	ultrasound

*Change pages. **Student B** will read the list below. **Student A** will write each item in the correct category.*

Student B:

X-rays	microscope	laser discs	satellites
smoke detectors	acupuncture	ibuprofen	binoculars
faxes	MRIs	seat belt	tapes

Unit 15, page 181

Student A: Turn to page 181.
Student B: Look at the sentences below. In each sentence, you both have different information about the same musician, singer, or composer. Listen to each other carefully. Together, try to write a new, longer sentence about each person, using an adjective clause.

Student B:

1. Elvis Presley was born in Mississippi.
2. Beethoven was a famous classical composer.
3. The Beatles had two lead singers and songwriters.
4. Duke Ellington was admired by many jazz performers.
5. Madonna is often controversial.
6. Janet Jackson's brothers were called the Jackson Five.

Tape Script

Unit 1, page 4

A. Listen: The University of Texas at San Antonio Listen to the description of this university. As you listen, circle or fill in the correct information.

The University of Texas is a large university with many campuses all over Texas. This is a description of the University of Texas at San Antonio, or U.T.S.A. U.T.S.A. is a four-year public university. U.T.S.A. is located on a suburban campus, fifteen miles from downtown San Antonio. It enrolls about 9,400 full-time students and 5,300 part-time students. It also has a graduate school of about 2,800 students. U.T.S.A. employs more than 700 faculty.

Students who want to attend U.T.S.A. pay a $40 application fee. The university recommends that high school students complete four years of English, two years of a foreign language, three years of math, two years of social science, and two years of science. They also recommend a year of fine arts.

U.T.S.A. has many majors to offer undergraduates: engineering, business, computers, foreign languages, history, music, art, and many others.

U.T.S.A. gives its students career counseling and has an employment service. For students who need extra help or preparation, there is a learning center with tutoring and special counselors. U.T.S.A. also provides special services for veterans and students with disabilities. For freshmen, there is a freshman orientation to inform the students about the university and its facilities.

Unit 2, page 23

A. Listen Look at the pairs of pictures and listen to the comparison between life in colonial times and life today. Then read each statement about colonial times. Circle T for true or F for false.

The colonial period in the United States lasted from 1607 to 1776. Most early colonists were men and women from England who decided to start a new life in North America. They settled along the eastern coast of what is now the United States, from Georgia to New Hampshire. Life at that time was very different from today. Most people lived on small farms and were self-sufficient for most of their needs. People grew all of their own food and cooked it over open fires. They didn't go to supermarkets or cook on stoves. When they needed milk, they milked their own cows. They didn't go to the supermarket and buy a carton of milk. Houses functioned without modern conveniences or electricity. Instead of electric lights, people read and worked by candlelight. They didn't sleep on mattresses with box springs. They used to sleep on feather beds. In the evening, instead of watching television, they read to each other and played games. When people wanted to communicate with friends or relatives far away, they used to write letters. They didn't have telephones or e-mail. For transportation, the people used horses and wagons; they didn't drive cars. Life was slower and simpler, but people worked hard from sun up to sun down.

Unit 3, page 36

A. Listen: *The divorce* Look at the pictures and listen to the story of Tom and Amy's divorce.

Amy and I were married twelve years ago. At one time, we were really happy together, at least I think we were. I don't know what happened. We've tried; we went to marriage counselors; we made promises, and then we broke them. It's just not working. Amy and I are going to get a divorce. I'm not worried about her or about myself; we're adults. I'm worried about the kids. We have two children, Carly and Jason. Carly is seven; Jason is ten. Amy and I have agreed on joint custody of the children. I'm packing tonight; I'm going to move to an apartment in the next town this weekend. Amy is going to stay here, in the house. The children are going to live with her during the week, and they're going to live with me on the weekends. They will still go to the same school and be with all their friends. In the summer, they'll live with me in July and with Amy in August. That way we can plan vacations and time with the kids.

Amy and I have made a lot of other agreements, too. I'm going to pay child support. And I'm going to pay alimony for seven years. We will divide our assets and our savings. Amy stayed home with the kids for years; she was a homemaker. She's going to need a job now. She finished one year of college before we got married. She'll go back to school part time and study accounting.

Life isn't going to be easy for any of us anymore. And I'm really going to miss being with the kids.

Unit 4, page 48

A. Listen: *Ali's neighborhood* Ali lives in an apartment in this neighborhood. The neighborhood has changed a lot in the past five years and he wants to move. Listen to his story and fill in the chart with the adjectives in the box. You can use two adjectives to describe some of the problems.

Ali's looking for a new apartment, but he's having a hard time. He likes the apartment, but he hates the neighborhood. The neighborhood has changed a lot in the last five years. It's not as nice as it used to be. In fact, it's more dangerous. There's more crime than there used to be, and it's not safe at night. He has three locks on his windows, too. And, the neighbors have changed. Ali's neighbors used to be really friendly, but they're not anymore. Most of the people he knew or he was friendly with have moved away. Now he has noisy neighbors who don't keep their apartments clean. One neighbor is in a band and he practices at night. Ali can't get to be a lot of convenience stores and groceries in that neighborhood, but now only a few are left. The prices are higher, so Ali has to shop in a different neighborhood. It's a lot of trouble! And, the streets and sidewalks are much dirtier than before. There never used to be garbage or litter on the street. Now, Ali always sees garbage bags on the street. In the summer, it smells terrible! Finally, Mr. Morales, the superintendent that Ali used to have, was much friendlier and more helpful. The new super, Mr. Johnson, isn't as friendly as Mr. Morales and he's not as helpful. He never fixes anything right away. Sometimes Ali has to wait for two weeks if there's a problem. Ali really needs to move as soon as possible.

page 52

H. Listen: *As...as* Listen to the information about two groceries in Ali's neighborhood. Fill in the missing adjective forms with (not) as _____ as.

Ali shops at two grocery stores in his neighborhood, the Green Market and the International Market.

Example 1: Ali likes to shop at the Green Market because the vegetables are fresh. The vegetables at the International Market are fresh, also.

Example 2: The prices at the International Market are average. The prices at the Green Market are always a few cents more.

1. Ali buys oranges at the Green Market because they are juicy. Ali also buys oranges at the International Market. They are juicy there, too.
2. The meat at both the Green Market and the International Market is delicious.
3. At the Green Market, the shelves are not crowded, so Ali can easily find things. At the International Market, the shelves are very crowded.
4. At the Green Market, the selection is limited. At the International Market, the selection is very large.
5. At the Green Market, and also at the International Market, the cashiers are very courteous and they always say "Hello" and "Thank you".
6. Ali likes the managers at both markets because they're very helpful.
7. When he needs a delivery, Ali always calls the Green Market because the delivery service is very quick.
8. Ali shops at the International Market more often because he pays less than at the Green Market.

Unit 5, page 60

A. Listen: The Yang family *You're going to hear a story about the Yang family. Listen and take notes about their ages, jobs, places of work or school, and interests.*

There are six members of the Yang family: William, 46, Patricia, 46, Charles, 42, Margaret, 20, Norman, 17, and Grandmother Yang, 67. They live in San Francisco, but they're originally from Hong Kong. They moved to San Francisco three years ago. The parents spoke English fluently when they arrived, so they were able to get work right away. William and Patricia are both professionals. William and Patricia work at the same hospital. William is an accountant in the business office, and Patricia is a nurse in the Emergency Room. Their oldest two children, Charles and Margaret are now college students. Charles is pre-med, and Margaret is studying architecture. Norman is in high school. The Yangs are very proud of their children. All of them are doing well in school, and Norman is captain of his high school baseball team. Grandmother Yang speaks English, too, and she volunteers in a library in Chinatown.

This summer, William and Patricia finally have enough money saved to take a vacation. The whole family is going to go to Vancouver, Canada, for the first time to visit William's younger brother, Victor.

page 61

B. Listen *Listen to the story about the Yang family again and check your notes. Then listen to each question and circle the correct answer.*

1. How old is William?
2. How old is the youngest child?
3. Where are the Yangs originally from?
4. When did they move to San Francisco?
5. Did everyone speak English when they arrived?
6. Where do William and Patricia work?
7. What does William do?
8. What does Patricia do?
9. What do Charles and Margaret do?
10. Is Norman good at baseball?
11. How does Grandmother Yang spend her time?
12. Where are they going to go this summer?

page 64

G. Listen: Tag questions *Listen and draw an arrow showing the correct intonation. Circle the verbs.*

Example

The Yangs are going to Canada, aren't they? ↘ **falling intonation**
(The speaker expects a "Yes" answer.)

You weren't born in Canada, were you? ↗ **rising intonation**
(The speaker isn't sure of the answer.)

1. The Yangs live in San Francisco, don't they?
2. Canada has two official languages, doesn't it?
3. Canada was first settled by the French, wasn't it?
4. Americans need identification to enter Canada, don't they?
5. Ice hockey is popular in Canada, isn't it?
6. Toronto isn't the capital of Canada, is it?
7. People in Quebec can't speak English, can they?
8. Niagara Falls isn't in Canada, is it?
9. There was a great fire in Vancouver in 1886, wasn't there?
10. Canada doesn't border Alaska, does it?

Unit 6, page 76

A. Listen: Retirement plans: will and may ack is going to retire next month. Listen to this conversation between Jack and a co-worker. *Complete each sentence with will/won't or may/might.*

Male 1: So, Jack, only one more week of work. What are your plans for retirement?
Male 2: I'm going to enjoy myself. I've always wanted to travel, and I'm going to. I'm taking a cruise to Alaska next month. After that, I'm not sure. I might go to Italy. Or I have a friend in Peru, and he's invited me to spend some time there.
Male 1: I hear you're thinking about selling your house.
Male 2: Yes. I need to paint it first, but I'm putting it on the market this summer.
Male 1: Will you stay in the area?
Male 2: I'm planning to. My daughter wants me to come to Florida and live with her. I might do that when I'm older. But for now, I'm going to look for an apartment or a condo. I have two brothers in the area, and my son lives in town, too.
Male 1: Do you still fish?
Male 2: You know, I haven't been fishing for years. I used to love to fish. I'm going to buy a new fishing rod and sit back and wait for a bite. I may even buy a small boat.
Male 1: Well, save some fish for me. I only have two more years here.

Unit 7, page 86

A. Listen: A driver's license Listen to Teresa, who hopes to get her driver's license soon. *Look at the chart and fill in the missing information about obtaining a license in her state.*

Teresa is looking for a part-time job, but there aren't many openings in her town. A friend of her father's will hire her to work in his office, but the company is about ten miles from her home. Teresa doesn't have a driver's license; she needs one by next month. Teresa plans to go to the Motor Vehicle Agency tomorrow to get a permit. In order to get her permit, Teresa has to take the written test and get at least 80% correct. There are thirty questions on the test. Her English isn't very good, but that's not a problem because the test is given in twenty languages. She has to pass a vision test, too. After she passes the two tests, Teresa has to pay $5.00 for her permit. In order to get the permit, she has to show proof of age. She can bring her birth certificate, her alien registration card, or her passport. When she has her permit, Teresa can practice driving for the road test, but only with a licensed driver. Her older brother promised to teach her how to drive, and her parents will drive with her on the weekends. On the day of her road test, her brother is going to drive her to the agency. She's going to use her brother's car and make sure she has her permit and the auto insurance card. She's nervous about the road test, but she needs to pass it so that she can get to her job.

page 88

E. Listen: Can and can't Listen to Marcus talk about his driving experience. *complete these sentences with can or can't.*

1. I can't drive very well.
2. I can drive only with a licensed driver in the car.
3. I can back up.
4. I can't parallel park.
5. I can't drive on a busy highway.

Unit 8, page 96

A. Listen: A phone call

Selma: Hi, Kathy. This is Selma.
Kathy: Kathy! How are you!? We haven't spoken for ages!
Selma: I know. We all get so busy. But have you heard? Angela's planning a family reunion.
Kathy: A family reunion! That's great! We haven't gotten together, all of us, for about five years. What is the date?
Selma: August. I think she said August 15th.
Kathy: August 15th. That's two months from now. And where's it going to be?
Selma: At Angela's. She's going to send out the invitations soon. And we'll all help and bring food.
Kathy: Of course. How many of us are there?
Selma: About seventy-five. Plus two more. My daughter, Jenny, just had twins. Two little girls. Identical twins.
Kathy: Beautiful! You're a grandmother! How's Jenny doing?
Selma: She's tired, but doing well. I help her out a few days a week.
Kathy: Did you hear that Michael has changed jobs?
Selma: No? Where's he working?
Kathy: He's opened a small business. He's putting companies on the Internet.
Selma: Wish him my best.
Kathy: I will. It'll be great to see everyone and hear what's happening.
Selma: See you in August.

Unit 9, page 109

C. Listen: A note from the boss.

Jeff: The boss wants to speak to me at 2:00. I left work early yesterday, but there was an emergency at home.
Katie: Well, is this the first time?
Jeff: Yes, I've never left early before.
Katie: And how about arriving on time?
Jeff: I've always arrived on time, and I've often stayed late.
Katie: Well, how are your sales figures?
Jeff: Great. I've written fifteen new car policies so far this month.
Katie: Have there been any complaints about you?
Jeff: Not that I know of. As a matter of fact, I've just received my latest evaluation, and it was very positive.
Katie: It doesn't sound like you've got anything to worry about. Maybe the boss wants to promote you!

C. Listen: a note from the boss *Jeff works for Careo Insurance. When he arrived at work this morning, there was a note on his e-mail asking him to see the boss at 2:00 this afternoon. Listen to his conversation with Katie, a co-worker. then complete these sentences about Jeff's job performance with the correct adverb.*

Unit 10, page 119

A. Listen: At the ballpark *Listen to a description of this minor league baseball game. Then read the statements below. Circle 'T' if the statement is True, 'F' if the statement is false.*

It's a Sunday afternoon in the summer. In Springfield, that means baseball. Every Saturday and Sunday afternoon, the local fans come out and watch their local minor league team play ball.

Today, the local team, the Stars, is playing the team from the next town. This is the game that the fans have been waiting for. The gate opened at 12:00. Angela has been selling tickets since then, and the fans are still coming in the gate. She's sold over eight hundred tickets so far.

The game started at 2:00. It is now in the 4th inning and it's not going well for the home team, which is trailing by a score of 3 to 1. The visitors have a new pitcher with a good fast ball. He has been striking out most of their players. And the home team has been making too many errors. But the game may be turning. The home team is at the plate. They have a player on second base, and their best hitter is up to bat. The fans are cheering and shouting. The local radio station is covering the game, and the announcer has been calling the game and describing every play.

Everyone in the concession stand has been working hard since the gate opened because the temperature is 95° and everyone is hot. Jason has been making Italian ices, and Mia and Ana have been serving soda and lemonade. Stanley has been walking up and down the stands, selling sodas. He's made twenty trips back to the concession stand for more sodas.

Unit 12, page 144

E. Listen: The first year Listen to each person talk about his or her decision to come to the United States and the first year in this country. Answer the questions below. Many include a gerund or an infinitive.

Speaker 1

I was worried about learning English. My brother wrote from the United States and he encouraged me to enroll me in English classes in my country, but I didn't. I regret not studying English before I got here, because for the first year, I couldn't understand anything and I always needed to have a translator with me whenever I went to the bank or the motor vehicle agency or to the store. Even now, two years later, I'm not that good at speaking English. I really don't enjoy studying, but I'm going to continue coming to school and trying to improve.

Speaker 2

Before we came here, I was concerned about finding a job. I was lucky. I'm good at fixing things and building, so I was able to find a job as a mason. We decided to come to the United States because of the opportunities. I admit having material-istic goals. I looked forward to buying things and doing things for my children. I dreamed about having a nice apartment and a car. I wanted to take my family on vacation, especially to Disneyworld. And now I can afford to send my daughters to piano lessons. In my country, you can work hard all your life and not have anything to show. I don't mind working long hours here, because we can get the things we want.

Speaker 3

I've been here for three years, and I still don't like the snow. I hate wearing a heavy coat. When it snows, it feels so cold and lonely. And it's hard to get around here if you don't have a car. I'm more comfortable taking the buses now, but at first I wasn't able to find the bus stops near my apartment or to get the schedules. But most of all, I missed, and I still miss, walking up and down the streets of my old city. In the United States, so much is new and many buildings are just plain and flat. In my country, the streets aren't straight. The building are hundreds of years old and the architecture is beautiful. I never appreciated the beauty of my city as much as I should have. We're returning to my country next summer and I plan on taking lots of photographs and bringing them back with me.

Unit 11, page 129

B. Listen: Personal dreams

Speaker 1

I have two boys, two teenagers. They're real good boys. They do very well in school. We expect them to study hard, and we encourage them to play sports and be involved in school activities. We want to send them to college. But it's difficult to save. We've been able to put some money in the bank, but it's not much. We want to see them both graduate from college someday.

Speaker 2

I've decided to start my own landscaping business. I live in Florida, and people have to maintain their yards here all year. There's lots of building around here, which I see as lots of potential customers. I work for a man now; we are able to take care of one hundred yards a week. I know how to cut and maintain lawns and how to start new lawns; I know the chemicals to apply and which plants grow well. But I don't have the capital. I need to buy a truck and the lawn equipment. Just last month, my brother offered to lend me $30,000. I've promised to pay him back in four years. I've started to speak to some new homeowners already. As soon as I have thirty customers, I'm going to buy the equipment.

Speaker 3

I don't have a dream in terms of accomplishing something big and special. I'd just love to have some time for myself. I work ten hours a day and I go to school, too, so every minute is taken up. I'd like to have time for a walk in the park every day. I want to read some love stories and some travel books. I'd like to talk to my friends on the telephone one night a week. My daughter asked me to volunteer in the school library, but I can't. That's it; my dream is one hour of free time a day.

Unit 13, page 155

C. **Listen: A product map** Look at the products on the bottom of page 154. Listen to the information about each product. Draw a line from the product to the state. When you finish, try to retell the information about each product.

1. **Kansas** Kansas is a flat state with rich soil. Much of the wheat that is grown in the United States is grown in Kansas.

2. **California** Motion pictures are produced in California. Hollywood, which is located in southern California, is known as the motion picture capital of the United States.

3. **South Dakota** Farm equipment, such as tractors and corn pickers, is manufactured in South Dakota.

4. **Oregon** Oregon is located on the Pacific Ocean, and fishing is a major industry. Salmon are caught and processed in Oregon.

5. **Utah** Utah is an important mining state. Copper, iron, and other minerals are mined from its mountains and canyons.

6. **Washington** The computer industry has provided thousands of new jobs, including the writing of computer software programs. Many of these new computer companies are located in the state of Washington.

7. **Oklahoma** Much of the rubber used in the United States and Canada is made of synthetic materials. Many rubber products, including tires, are manufactured in Oklahoma.

8. **Arizona** Because of its warm weather, Arizona has a long growing season. Lettuce is grown there many months of the year.

Unit 14, page 166

C. **Listen: Famous structures** Listen to these descriptions of three of the structures in the pictures. Complete the chart with short notes, then answer the questions.

First, let's look at the pyramids. The pyramids are some of the oldest structures on the earth. Most of the pyramids are located near the Nile River in Egypt. These giant structures were built more than two thousand years ago as tombs for Egyptian kings. The dead person was buried deep within the pyramid. The Egyptians believed that the dead person's spirit needed the same things as a living person. Therefore, all the person's valuable belongings and large amounts of food and water were buried with the body. The largest pyramid is called the Great Pyramid, which covers over 13 acres and stands 481 feet high. It took 100,000 slaves 20 years to build this pyramid.

Next, the Taj Mahal is a monument to love. This majestic structure was built in India in 1648. The emperor at that time greatly loved his wife, Mumtaz Mahal, who died in 1631 while giving birth to their fourteenth child. In her honor, the emperor ordered the construction of the most beautiful tomb in the world. The large central area and side rooms are covered by a magnificent dome. The structure is surrounded by beautiful pools and gardens.

The third structure on the chart, the Eiffel Tower, was erected in Paris, France, in 1889. It was built for an exhibition celebrating the hundredth anniversary of the French Revolution. All of the parts of this tower were pre-made of the highest quality iron, and then they were numbered. They arrived in Paris, and the workers put them together as if they were putting together a giant puzzle, trying to make all the pieces fit.

Unit 15, page 176

A. Listen: Country music *Listen to the history of country music. Then circle T for true, or F for false.*

The people who first sang the country sound lived over a hundred years ago in the Appalachian Mountains. These people sang all the time, while they were working, while they were doing laundry, while at church, or while they were taking care of their babies. People used to sing to make the work go faster. The music that they sang was very simple.

The music, which is called country music, came from the British Isles: Scotland, Ireland, England, and Wales. The people who migrated to this country, moved to a land that was similar to their homeland. The people brought their music with them.

Two instruments were common in country music bands. The five-string banjo, which came from Africa, became popular in country music in the 1920s. The fiddle, which had early roots in Nashville, was the main instrument in country music until the 1930s. The fiddler, who carried the melody, was usually the main performer in country music bands. Banjos and fiddles are still popular in country music bands today, but other instruments, such as electric guitars and keyboards, are also used. Jimmy Rodgers and the Carter family, who first recorded in 1927, became the first superstars of country music.

page 178

D. Listen: When and where as relative pronouns *Listen to the information on the tape about singer Mary Chapin Carpenter and fill in the missing information in the sentences below.*

Example 1: Mary Chapin Carpenter won five WAMMYs in 1986.

Example 2: She moved to Washington after graduation and wrote many original songs there.

1. Mary Chapin Carpenter lived in Tokyo for two years because her father worked for a magazine.
2. When Carpenter was in school in Connecticut, she met Joan Baez, a famous folk singer.
3. She went to college at Brown University and continued to sing and write songs.
4. After 1981, she moved back to Washington, D.C., and started to play at coffeehouses and clubs.
5. She was discovered in a Washington club by a recording studio executive.
6. In 1987, her first album was released.
7. In 1990, she won a Grammy Award for one of her songs.